I would like to dedicate my part of the book to my daughters Jessica, Di and Amy, who have taught me so much more than I could teach them.

Sue Colverd

I would like to dedicate my part of the book to Maria.

Bernie Hodgkin

Developing Emotional Intelligence in the Primary School

Do you want to promote sociability and positive behaviour in your classroom? Is having an "emotionally intelligent classroom" one of your teaching goals? Are you looking for ways to teach the curriculum more "creatively"?

Developing Emotional Intelligence in the Primary School is an essential text for supporting children's emotional preparation for learning in the long term, fostering the development both of self-belief and permanent and crucial resilience.

This book allows teachers to review their practice and approach to teaching and to reassess how they view their pupils. Using practical drama frames that teachers can develop for themselves, it gives a background and framework to build emotional intelligence in a child and generate a culture of openness to learning in the classroom.

Areas covered include:

- Self-esteem, emotional and social intelligence;
- Independence and self-reliance;
- Creating an emotionally intelligent learning environment;
- Emotional literacy based around core curriculum areas including literacy and science;
- Conflict resolution and anti-bullying strategies;
- Using and integrating positional drama for emotional intelligence.

With a number of practical techniques and activities to be implemented in the classroom, this introduction to emotional intelligence will be of great interest to all primary schoolteachers looking to further their understanding of pupils' social and emotional development through learning.

Sue Colverd has worked in educational and theatre settings for thirty years as a director, practitioner, writer and lecturer. She is Senior Lecturer in Drama and Theatre at the University of Gloucestershire.

Bernard Hodgkin is currently working for Herefordshire LA within the School Improvement and Inclusion team. He has worked in a wide variety of educational settings over a thirty-five year career as a teacher in schools and further and higher education, including leading Initial Teacher Training programmes.

Developing Emotional Intelligence in the Primary School

Sue Colverd and
Bernard Hodgkin

Routledge
Taylor & Francis Group

LONDON AND NEW YORK

First edition published 2011
by Routledge
2 Park Square, Milton Park, Abingdon, Oxon OX14 4RN

Simultaneously published in the USA and Canada
by Routledge
270 Madison Avenue, New York, NY 10016

Routledge is an imprint of the Taylor & Francis Group, an informa business

Typeset in Bembo by
Florence Production Ltd, Stoodleigh, Devon
Printed and bound in Great Britain by
TJ International Ltd, Padstow, Cornwall

British Library Cataloguing in Publication Data
A catalogue record for this book is available from the British Library

Library of Congress Cataloging-in-Publication Data
Colverd, Sue.
   Developing emotional intelligence in the primary school: a practical
   guide for teachers/Sue Colverd and Bernard Hodgkin.
      p. cm.
   Includes bibliographical references and index.
   1. Behavior modification—Great Britain.   2. Emotional intelligence
   —Great Britain.   3. Child psychology—Great Britain.   4. Education
   (Elementary)—Great Britain.   I. Hodgkin, Bernard.   II. Title.
   LB1060.2.C65 2011
   370.15′34—dc22   2010030553

ISBN13: 978-0-415-56943-9 (hbk)
ISBN13: 978-0-415-56946-0 (pbk)
ISBN13: 978-0-203-83316-2 (ebk)

Contents

Illustrations

Figures

Tables

Acknowledgements

My thanks go to the following people: Bernie, my inspirational friend, who suggested we should write this book; Debbie Sleep, her staff and the children at Stroud Valley Community School for allowing us to develop with them new drama work and approaches, and for their great enthusiasm and support; teachers Suzanne Boston, Sarah Roberts, Kate Hawkins and Helen Richardson who incorporated our drama techniques and developed ideas in the classroom, giving us invaluable feedback; Carol Baron, her staff and the children of Uplands Primary School for piloting the *Super Me* Project. Many thanks for all the pre-project planning and ongoing support. Thanks to Katy Nicol for her great insight and support in developing our work with vulnerable young people. Grateful thanks are due, also, to Sarah Coldrick, Kate Littlewood, Neil Colverd and Linda Miles for their continued encouragement, belief and support; practitioners Jude Emmet and Louise Partridge for their invaluable practical input into the *Super Me* Project; Celia Balbernie and Gloucestershire Social Services; the University of Gloucestershire; and the team at Routledge, who have been so supportive to us in the publication of our work.

Sue Colverd

My thanks to Sue, my co-author, for her consistent and continued diligence, intelligence and wit; my son and daughter, Kieran and Cerys, for their support, their inspiration and their energy; Michael Barrett, of Ballina, Co. Mayo in Ireland, for his support and belief; Sarah Coldrick for her continual support and her wonderful suppers; Jonothan Neelands, Dorothy Heathcote and Essex University for their support all those years ago; teachers as participants on the MEd Professional Development (Drama) course at the University of Gloucestershire, 2006 to 2008; Dorothy Bolland, my critical friend, for her interest, her belief and her sense of humour; Mike Francis; and Auntie Olwen, for her Welsh cakes and moral support. I must also thank former pupils/students from: The Ockendon School, South Ockendon, Essex (formerly Culverhouse School); Archway School,

Stroud, Gloucestershire; National Star College, Cheltenham, Gloucestershire; South Gloucestershire Pupil Referral Unit, Mangotsfield, Bristol; Young People's Support Services, Wiltshire; Cleeve School, Cheltenham, Gloucestershire; the University of Gloucestershire, Cheltenham. And of course Mum and Dad, and all my family, close friends and colleagues too numerous to mention: THANK YOU.

Bernie Hodgkin

How to Use this Book

This book has been written as a tool for teachers to use in their everyday delivery in the classroom. Chapters 1, 2 and 3 provide a basis for understanding the foundations needed for emotional security in children, and explores reasons why some children exhibit erratic, challenging or puzzling behaviours in the classroom, through theories of motivation, attachment, learning, and emotional and social intelligence. All of these theories are practically applied to the classroom and school environment, and to teaching styles and delivery.

Chapters 4, 5, 6, 7 and 8 explain practical creative, drama-based techniques and specific models – relating back to the issues explored in Chapters 1, 2 and 3. The working drama models are all written with follow-up ideas so that they may be used as a basis for development. The Positional Drama models are all complete for the areas they cover, (i.e. creative writing, history and PSHE), so you may use them without referring back to the initial overall description.

We would advise you, when integrating the drama models into your practice, to refer back to the theories occasionally to keep the practical approaches in context.

Introduction

Primary teachers are being asked, increasingly, to deliver learning for the "whole child" and for children's specific needs and learning styles. They are also being asked to facilitate "emotional literacy/intelligence" to control and promote sociability and positive behaviour; to use drama and "role play"; and to facilitate the curriculum "creatively". Teachers need a strong framework to underpin a new approach to delivering learning in a creative and emotionally intelligent way. We will need to review our practical approach to teaching and reassess how we work with our pupils.

The aim of this book is to give a background and framework to what is required to build emotional intelligence in the primary school and how the practical use of integrated drama can breed a culture of safety and openness to learning in the classroom. We have worked with committed and talented educators who confirm that our approach has invigorated their teaching and assisted them to use drama creatively to incorporate emotional intelligence approaches for learning and support behaviour in their teaching.

The aim of this approach to teaching is to enable children to recognise and understand their feelings, and so become more adept at handling and expressing them. It is accepted that children who are less unduly stressed are able to manage competing demands more effectively. Emotionally literate children will acquire, as a result, an increased attention span, and subsequently gain greater prowess at forming and maintaining relationships. As teachers,

> However many years we have been teaching we can always benefit from some reflection on our teaching and management practice.
>
> If we are willing, and see a need for change in our management practice, and if we are aware of more effective management we can always learn with support.

Developing emotional literacy in children should be carried out in tandem with developing emotional literacy among staff.

Self-efficacy should be seen as the trigger for the enhancement of emotional literacy among staff – self-efficacy defined as "a belief we hold as to how far we will be able to achieve success in a particular area".

It may be argued that the teachers who are most effective in dealing with misbehaviour are those most confident in their ability to teach challenging children. It follows that teachers high in self-efficacy are more likely to use positive teaching strategies such as praise, modifying their teaching approaches and encouraging and praising children for the effort they make in their work.

Teachers need to be aware that positive or negative behaviour is not a choice but a consequence of a child's "expectations of adults", expectations that the child has learnt through life experiences. The teacher must view the children in the light of life outside the school as well as how they present themselves in the classroom. The teacher is being directed to provide social and emotional learning that, we would argue, cannot be taught in blocks with specific lesson plans but day-by-day through the relationship and understanding that is built between teacher and pupil. This approach needs a school ethos that seeks to know and understand the children under its care through different perspectives. The delivery of learning by the teacher, in both practical and personal terms, is paramount to the child's engagement and behaviour.

Why do some children engage easily with the learning process while others remain disconnected from it? What makes some children secure in themselves and in you as their facilitator *in loco parentis*,[1] ready to embrace knowledge and new experiences, while others treat you as "the enemy", seemingly wanting to sabotage your plans and the learning of their peers? Once we begin to understand the issues and processes that might be contributing to challenging or non-engaged behaviour, we will be able to gain fresh perspectives. Where we feel challenged or made to feel inadequate in our teaching ability, we can try different approaches and formulate strategies to become more confident in our skills and our teaching powers.

It is important to analyse how we see ourselves as educators, how the children see us, and how we view the children; how the teacher influences positive and negative behaviour. What can be done to improve the learning experience for the pupil and the teacher, and how does this impact upon learning? How can we continuously invigorate and develop our practice?

This book gives an insight into, a basis for, and examples of how to facilitate these approaches, long term, in the inclusive classroom. The inclusive classroom may be defined as one which, with a continuing emphasis on individual differences and irrespective of social or cultural background, disability or difficulty in learning, leads all pupils to succeed in the fulfilment of their academic goals, and in their development of positive attitudes to themselves and others.

The insights into and understanding of how to control behaviour and encourage sociability and emotional intelligence, through a creative teaching approach, make this a practical handbook. The models in it are a basis and a template for teachers to use and upon which to develop their skills.

The Secure Base: Attachment to Learning

Priorities in practice

The education community is ever changing and, following publication of the *Every Child Matters* agenda, there has emerged a much stronger emphasis on the individual child and the role of the support agencies in preparing the child for learning in a positive and safe environment. The SEAL[1] directive encourages teachers to progress the child's social and emotional development.

To facilitate this development, it is vital to understand how the child functions and what helps and hinders the process of learning, emotions, empathy and sociability in a child's development. Chapter 1 will explore some of the body of knowledge we have on the effects that environment and parenting have on a child's development and attachment to learning. We will be applying these theories to classroom strategies and techniques for delivery.

Perhaps the most challenging issue for teachers in their day-to-day life in the classroom is managing behaviour. When we teach we make an agreement with the students that they give the teaching their attention. Without attention, whatever your teaching style, the learning cannot take place to its full potential. A distracting child pulls focus on to his or her needs. When this builds to two or three or more behavioural issues in a classroom, a teacher is seriously hampered in their delivery, which can be extremely frustrating and demoralising. At these points the teacher needs to be able to step back, see and understand the child, and put in place strategies to help focus and contain the behaviour. The child must not become the focus of the teacher's frustration and be perceived as disrupting by choice. This gives the child too much power and can lead to confrontations that might give the child the attention he or she craves. Confrontation should always be avoided, since it promotes a negative atmosphere that affects the whole class and can disempower the teacher. The strategy should always be to change the state of the child and the negative energy that the child may be building in him- or herself or trying to instil in you.

In an American film called *Boys Town* (1938: dir. Norman Taurog), based on the true story of Father Flanagan, a priest opens a school for a group of disadvantaged and delinquent boys in a home that he founded and named Boys Town. The boys elect their own government and a mayor, and they agree on rules and punishments, creating their own social structure. Father Flanagan has a maxim: "There are no bad boys. There is only bad environment, bad training, bad example, bad thinking."[2]

In today's society we read headlines that seek to "name and shame" children who have perpetrated crimes or hurt other children. Often children are seen in the media as either victims ("angels") or perpetrators ("demons"). Children who brutalise other children often have histories of being brutalised themselves, through physical, emotional and sexual abuse, and in witnessing terrible degrees of domestic violence. Yet we rarely see headlines that empathise with the perpetrator, although the perpetrators themselves are also children. We need to use our emotional intelligence to understand our feelings in relation to the event and employ our rationale to distance our emotions from our reason. If we do not see the perpetrators of child–upon–child acts of violence as children who have learnt their behaviour from their nurture and environment, we do not give ourselves the opportunity to plan strategies for change. In a far less extreme scenario there is the behaviour of the children in our classrooms, behaviour that will be affected by their experience of life and the adults who have reared them. Our response to them needs to be strategic and not emotional, even when their disruptions can push our patience and our resources to the limit.

Domestic violence accounts for 14 per cent of all violent incidents in England and Wales. It has more repeat victims than any other crime: repeat victimisation accounts for 66 per cent of all incidents of domestic violence and 21 per cent of victims have been victimised three or more times (Walker *et al.* 2009). In fact, research demonstrating the emotionally harmful effects upon children of witnessing domestic abuse or violence is now part of the threshold criteria, the criteria that courts need to satisfy themselves of before making a care order.[3] Over a quarter (26 per cent) of young adults reported that physical violence sometimes took place between those caring for them during childhood. For 5 per cent this violence was constant or frequent. In 75 per cent of cases mothers reported that their children had directly witnessed domestic violence. Thirty-three per cent had seen their mothers beaten and 10 per cent had witnessed sexual violence (UK Action for Children 1994). In a study by the NSPCC, *Living with Significant Harm*, research evidence highlighted the detrimental, complex, entrenched and damaging effects which domestic violence has upon children's health and development (Brandon *et al.* 2005). These statistics are shocking, but when we look at them we begin to understand that some of the children in our classes may be experiencing violent and unsafe home lives.

There are many children who are suffering abuse, neglect and bereavement, witnessing domestic violence and family breakdown, living with parents with mental health problems, caring for parents, and suffering from confusion, pain, anger and stress. Consequently their behaviour will reflect their emotional situation and they can be challenging, puzzling and infuriating. The school environment, and you as their adult role model who is perceived as kind, positive and caring, may represent their only chance of being rescued from a negative pattern of learnt behaviour.

Do we believe that the challenging child, who continually expresses him- or herself through difficult and unacceptable behaviour, is happy or content? Do we believe that a child does not want to be liked, respected, to have fun and friends, and to be successful in our school environment? Do we believe in the "bad" boy or girl? If we do, then building strategies to try to help that child becomes very difficult; we are angry with the "choices" we feel they are making. They stop us teaching, and prevent their peers from learning. We need to understand where the behaviour has been seeded, to empathise with this, and, if we can, to help the child grow in other directions and see the benefits of other behaviours. We are being asked to facilitate the emotional life of the children in our care, to regulate their behaviour (which is a consequence of their emotions), to be able to control and analyse their emotions when they have an adverse effect on behaviour; so we must analyse what our understanding of emotional intelligence is and how we value and use it.

The school environment and ethos is crucial to this. It is the child's "other home" – a model that should reflect the safe base of the positive, nurturing home environment. It needs to become a safe alternative for the vulnerable child: to represent the possibility of a safe, caring environment in which the child can experience the good home, with positive, nurturing, adult role models, and can access not only an academic experience but a social and emotional life-enhancing one.

So let us begin with an open mind and look at environment, using the framework of Maslow's Hierarchy of Needs to help us focus on what the school should provide to be safe and to motivate its learning family.

The Hierarchy of Needs applied to a child's learning (Abraham Maslow)

Abraham Maslow was born in New York in 1908. He was one of seven children and was encouraged by his uneducated parents, Jewish immigrants from Russia, to achieve academic success. He studied psychology and received his BA in 1930, his MA in 1931 and his PhD in 1934 at the University of Wisconsin. This formed the basis of his motivational research. Maslow became leader of the Humanistic School of Psychology that emerged in the 1950s and 1960s, which he referred to as the "third force", beyond Freudian theory and behaviourism.

Maslow developed his original five-stage Hierarchy of Needs model in mid-twentieth-century America for understanding human motivation and personal development. The Hierarchy of Needs has been applied as a model for the progression of human well-being and development in a healthy, nurturing society. The Hierarchy is shown as a staged pyramid, with a series of steps towards "self-actualisation". Each step of the Hierarchy must be achieved before the individual can progress to the next level; if the needs are not met, the progression does not happen or it becomes fractured.

The five steps are as follows:

- *Biological and Physiological Needs*: shelter – food and drink – warmth – sleep
- *Safety Needs*: protection – security – order – limits – stability
- *Belonging and Love Needs*: family – affection – relationships
- *Esteem Needs*: achievement – status – responsibility – reputation
- *Self-actualisation*: personal growth and fulfilment

Maslow's Hierarchy of Needs is used in management and marketing strategies around the world to empower companies' management systems in the way they structure their businesses to motivate their employees. The Hierarchy has become a basis for structuring models to aid an individual's or group's process of personal development and progression. The stages of the Hierarchy link to the aims of the *Every Child Matters* agenda: to be healthy and achieve economic well-being (Biological and Physiological Needs); to stay safe (Safety Needs); to enjoy and achieve (Esteem Needs); and to make a positive contribution (Self-actualisation).

Let us look at a model that uses the theory of the Hierarchy of Needs to motivate the people who work in a business. The business could be one that produces buttons or computers, or it could be a school; both need a structure to nurture and work with their staff.

Biological and Physiological Needs

The initial steps are fulfilling the basic needs of drink, food, warmth, shelter and sleep: biological and physiological needs that must be met for us to survive. If a person goes into their workplace and it is cold through lack of heating, the roof is leaking, the food in the canteen is awful or too expensive, then their basic needs are not being met. They will not function, or they will function, but only grudgingly; they will not be motivated to stay.

Safety Needs

Employees need to feel a sense of safety. They need to know the rules and what is required of them. When a person feels safe and secure, they can relax and focus on the task in hand.

Belonging and Love Needs

When "safety" is in place, the employer needs to facilitate a sense of "belonging". When an employee connects to an organisation or company, a sense of being part of a team and working towards a shared goal is engendered. An organisation might structure itself as a family, nurturing its staff, who will be loyal and work hard in return. On a fundamental level, this might be achieved through good catering facilities, comfortable workspaces and good holiday provision. Staying with the company entitles the employees to company breaks and activities, good training opportunities and other work incentives. Employees who do gain a sense of belonging to their company work in a positive and generous way, and they might say "I *love* working here!"

Esteem Needs

When employees feel they "belong" in the organisation and work well, their managers must find positive means of expressing their value to the organisation by, for example, structuring progression pathways, building responsibilities and positive feedback so that employees feel they can develop and grow within the workplace. A sense of importance and value is crucial to motivation, making people feel there is a reason to work hard and improve.

Self-actualisation

When all the steps in the Hierarchy are in place, employees will be motivated to take responsibility for their own development. They will become valued, motivated, loyal members of the workforce. They might even move into management.

The Hierarchy of Needs gives a firm structure to the understanding of how a person feels when coming into a new environment, and how the management could motivate them through the structures they put in place within their organisation.

Maslow's Hierarchy of Needs is a great tool to help us build a safe, motivational world for children starting out in an educational establishment. They are coming into a "workplace", one that is new and alien to them. If a school is working with this structure for its staff, and the staff have reached "Self-actualisation" and are secure, well supported, confident in their teaching ability, motivated and understand how powerful the stages of the Hierarchy of Needs are to development, they are in a strong position to structure a safe and progressive social learning environment for the children in their care.

The Hierarchy of Needs in relation to your pupil

The child needs to know that this workplace will provide for their biological and physiological needs. They need to know they will be warm, be cared for if they are unwell or hurt themselves, where the toilet is and be able to use it when they need it, and where to get food and drink.

The child needs to have a structure that allows them to be and feel safe and secure in their new environment. They need to know who the adults in their environment are, and to trust the adults to be able to keep them safe. And this will apply to each change of classroom, teacher and teaching assistant throughout their school years.

The child needs to connect with or attach to the workplace. This includes environment and people. They need to attach to their teacher and connect with other children. They need to feel they are liked, are part of the larger group, and that they belong to this place. It is another nurturing family environment (or it might be their only model of a nurturing family environment).

The child needs to feel they are important and valued in the workplace, that they can be entrusted with tasks that are achievable, and that they have status within their peer groups and with their teachers.

The child needs to be able to leave that workplace with a strong sense of who they are and an ability to develop and realise new skills and achievements. They need to be self-reliant enough to be motivated in and meet the expectations of the next workplace.

Let us look at an example of the Hierarchy of Needs' five stages as they might be applied to a child's journey through school (Figure 1.1). The first stage at the

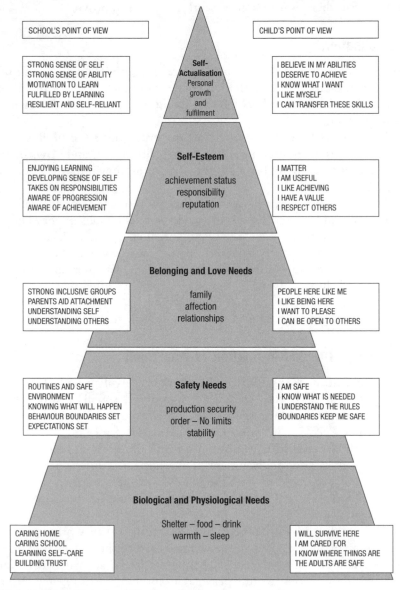

FIGURE 1.1 Maslow's Hierarchy of Needs applied to children's learning

foot of the triangle represents their first experience in Reception. They then begin their journey through the stages, each one giving the child the necessary structure of safety, trust and self-belief to aspire to achieve the next stage. The safety level represented by the teacher and the class in each new year group must fulfil the safety needs of the child afresh. For example, if a child moves from Reception to Year 1 and has a negative experience of their new teacher or of the classroom environment, their learning may regress if their safety needs are no longer being met.

As we know, all children are unique and will move through these stages at different paces. Several factors will be involved in this: home environment, the child's sense of safety, the school environment, parenting, the wider family and teaching. As you look at this version of the Hierarchy, you will no doubt recognise behaviours and be able to place your pupils at their various stages. It will be probable that you have pupils who are at different stages of the Hierarchy in the same class. We have given the teacher's view of the pupil through the stages, and the pupil's view of him or herself. The stages do not denote school years; a child's progression through the stages will happen within their personal development at different times.

Classroom needs for a child to feel safe to function

> The healthy spontaneous child, in his spontaneity, from within out, in response to his own inner Being, reaches out to the environment in wonder and interest, and expresses whatever skills he has.
>
> (Maslow 1968)

We can observe and recognise the positive progression of a child, who comes from a safe and secure home environment in which they are nurtured and valued, moving into the further safe, secure and nurturing environment of a primary school with a strong child–centred ethos.

They are able to progress through the stages and build on their sense of self and self-reliance. As they progress, they connect with (or attach to) their teachers and, via them, to the learning. They develop a sense of belonging to the school family; they have a role and a status. They become a "valued member of the class"; they behave well and respond well. They take on responsibility and are empowered by the school environment. They function well as a social member of the school community. They become a successful, fulfilled child with a strong potential to grow into a successful, fulfilled adult.

The school is able to work with the child and the parent to build on confidence and resilience. The parent can aid their child's sense of belonging by positive affirmation of the school and its teachers, helping the child to feel safe and to connect with the learning experience. Maslow states, in the above quote, what the healthy, spontaneous child is capable of as they reach out to their environment, but this is dependent upon the child not being crippled by fear to the extent that he or she does not feel "safe enough to dare" (Maslow 1968).

But what happens when the child is not supported by a safe home environment? We know that, in 2009, 4 million children (almost one-third of all children) were living in poverty, and that of those, 1.7 million were living in severe and persistent poverty. Growing up in poverty can have a severe effect on children's health and well-being and success at school (Save the Children 2010).

By the age of 6, a less able child from a rich family is likely to have overtaken an able child born into a poor family (Sharma 2007).

Domestic violence (as we have already noted) accounts for one in seven (14 per cent) of all violent incidents (Walker *et al.* 2009), and children often witness this in their own homes. Sixteen per cent of children experience serious maltreatment by parents, of whom one-third experience more than one type of maltreatment (Cawson 2002). Seven per cent of children experienced serious physical abuse at the hands of their parents or carers during childhood. Six per cent of children experienced serious absence of care at home during childhood. Six per cent of children experienced frequent and severe emotional maltreatment during childhood. One per cent of children experienced sexual abuse by a parent or carer and a further 3 per cent by another relative during childhood. Eleven per cent of children experienced sexual abuse by people known but unrelated to them. Five per cent of children experienced sexual abuse by an adult stranger or someone whom they had just met (Cawson 2002).

We can see from these statistics that many children live in a home environment that does not meet their physiological, biological and safety needs, and this will be reflected in their behaviour, their resilience and their ability to learn. How do these children manage the stages of the hierarchy? What are we likely to see from these children regarding behaviour and the ability to progress and attach to the learning experience that the school wants to provide?[4]

If we apply the "Learning Family" metaphor to the school experience, we are seeing ourselves either as surrogates, in place of the family, during the child's time with us, or as part of an extended family that the child experiences, hopefully, in all its wonder and interest (Maslow 1968). The family unit, whether it be one parent, two parents, large, small, functional or dysfunctional, is the child's main frame of reference. The child's expectation of life and adults has been structured in their brains by their experience of life and adults up until this point.

When we study the work-based motivational usage of Maslow's Hierarchy of Needs we see clearly the need to create a structured, nurturing workplace that holds, encourages and motivates its employees to get the best work from them. The headteacher, the teacher and the teaching assistant must manage the vulnerability of children who come into a new school and then, every year, move to a new class, and must set about building structures that allow children to attach to and function well and happily within their new "Learning Family". A child needs to be supported to feel they can belong to their extended school family. This ability to attach to the learning is critical for the learning process. The school must offer safety, care and experiences that will develop the child's social, emotional and learning potential.

Vulnerable children are likely to have a low tolerance level in any situation that will stress them. If they do become stressed they are likely to not be able

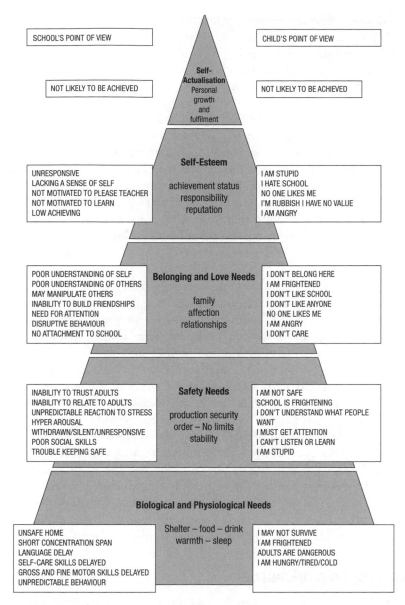

SCHOOL'S POINT OF VIEW

CHILD'S POINT OF VIEW

NOT LIKELY TO BE ACHIEVED

NOT LIKELY TO BE ACHIEVED

Self-Actualisation
Personal
growth
and
fulfilment

Self-Esteem

achievement status
responsibility
reputation

UNRESPONSIVE
LACKING A SENSE OF SELF
NOT MOTIVATED TO PLEASE TEACHER
NOT MOTIVATED TO LEARN
LOW ACHIEVING

I AM STUPID
I HATE SCHOOL
NO ONE LIKES ME
I'M RUBBISH I HAVE NO VALUE
I AM ANGRY

Belonging and Love Needs

family
affection
relationships

POOR UNDERSTANDING OF SELF
POOR UNDERSTANDING OF OTHERS
MAY MANIPULATE OTHERS
INABILITY TO BUILD FRIENDSHIPS
NEED FOR ATTENTION
DISRUPTIVE BEHAVIOUR
NO ATTACHMENT TO SCHOOL

I DON'T BELONG HERE
I AM FRIGHTENED
I DON'T LIKE SCHOOL
I DON'T LIKE ANYONE
NO ONE LIKES ME
I AM ANGRY
I DON'T CARE

Safety Needs

production security
order – No limits
stability

INABILITY TO TRUST ADULTS
INABILITY TO RELATE TO ADULTS
UNPREDICTABLE REACTION TO STRESS
HYPER AROUSAL
WITHDRAWN/SILENT/UNRESPONSIVE
POOR SOCIAL SKILLS
TROUBLE KEEPING SAFE

I AM NOT SAFE
SCHOOL IS FRIGHTENING
I DON'T UNDERSTAND WHAT PEOPLE WANT
I MUST GET ATTENTION
I CAN'T LISTEN OR LEARN
I AM STUPID

Biological and Physiological Needs

Shelter – food – drink
warmth – sleep

UNSAFE HOME
SHORT CONCENTRATION SPAN
LANGUAGE DELAY
SELF-CARE SKILLS DELAYED
GROSS AND FINE MOTOR SKILLS DELAYED
UNPREDICTABLE BEHAVIOUR

I MAY NOT SURVIVE
I AM FRIGHTENED
ADULTS ARE DANGEROUS
I AM HUNGRY/TIRED/COLD

FIGURE 1.2 Maslow's Hierarchy of Deficiency applied to children's learning

to regulate their anxiety. They are likely to not understand what is required from them and to have limited language and self-care skills. They may become angry or aggressive, they may freeze or behave unpredictably. They may exhibit confusing behaviour for no apparent reason, or not want to talk or enter into a social situation.

Let us use the Hierarchy to consider the likelihood of a child from an unsafe home environment with a low level of parent input being able to attain the stages, investigating their feelings and the teacher's perception of their behaviour.

When a child's needs are not met, their ability to move through the Hierarchy of Needs can be severely limited. Figure 1.2 is an extreme scenario, but if primary adult carers are unpredictable or unsafe, then the child will have no reason to believe other adults or situations to be safe, and he or she will take much longer to feel safe in the school environment.

> We fostered two little boys. They had been with us for a few days when I was giving them tea and I put the plate on the table over one of the boy's shoulders and he ducked and covered his head with his arms. We knew they had been in a violent home but I was very shocked because he thought I was going to hit him. Then you realise that there's no reason why these children should trust you, because their parents weren't to be trusted. All adults are the same to them. It takes a very long time to stop those triggers happening. Trust is broken at such a deep level.
>
> Carer (2009)

For many children who come from unsafe backgrounds, learning will not take place until the child feels secure in a safe environment. The child will spend time in fear, or watching for the adults to do something unsafe – as did the adults in the child's home environment. Any change in their class routine or environment, such as a new adult coming into the classroom, an unexpected change of routine or a fire drill, might trigger a high stress reaction.[5]

It is essential to acknowledge that, when a child comes into the Reception classroom, they have a head start or are weighed down by the level of nurture and care they have received in the home environment. This can often be seen in the demeanour, the behaviour, the hyper-vigilance or watchfulness and the physical appearance of the child. Sometimes a lack of care and safety can exist in families where that lack is not so visibly evident. The question remains the same, however, whatever the degree of emotional or physiological deprivation: how can the school environment have a profound impact upon the emotional development of its children? How can it "reel in" those children who are not going to attach easily to teachers, rules, routine, other children and learning?

The school as a role model

If a child can feel safe, cared for and nurtured in the school environment, then the step leading to belonging and connectedness might be achieved. The school becomes the "good parent", who will nurture and keep the child safe. The school invites the child into its safe social world, with trusted adults, clear routines and boundaries, and imaginative and creative approaches to learning that will help the child to re-pattern their expectation of what their world can be like. The school will be the model that shows the child alternative boundaries, behaviours and expectations.

For the well-adjusted child, who is nurtured and secure in the home environment, the safe transition into the school environment is an invaluable beginning to the possibilities of learning what this new world can offer.

This will not be easy, though, with a child who expects uncaring, unpredictable or unsafe behaviour from adults. The child might have very poor social and processing skills and, although the Reception class might be forewarned about the arrival of a vulnerable and challenging child, it does not necessarily make it easier to accommodate that child's needs or manage their behaviour. The greater the needs or the trauma of the child the more challenging and unpredictable the behaviour will be. Parents often have a negative attitude towards school originating from their own experience, and this can be transmitted to the child, and in such a case the teacher needs to win the parents' confidence and belief in order to help them engage in their child's learning. In some cases the school needs to act *in loco parentis* to both the child and its parent.

Let us look at the child's relationship with their carer and how this affects their development and the strength of their attachment to their school community and learning. To understand why children develop their behaviours in the ways that they do, we will look at what happens as a child develops with and without a "secure base".

Bowlby – Attachment Theory

Dr John Bowlby was born in London in 1907. He studied medicine at Trinity College, Cambridge, and moved into psychology in his final year, graduating in 1928. He spent a year teaching in two boarding-schools, one of which was a school for disturbed children. He became medically qualified in 1933 and then went to the Maudsley Hospital to train in adult psychiatry. After the Second World War, when he was an army psychiatrist, he moved to the Tavistock Clinic and became director of the Department for Children and Parents. Here he focused his clinical studies on the effects of mother–child separation. He completed a monograph for the World Health Organisation on the fate of homeless children in post-war Europe, "Maternal Care and Mental Health", and collaborated with James Robertson on a film, *A Two-year-old Goes to Hospital*. These works drew the attention of child clinicians to the potentially devastating effects of maternal separation, and led to the liberalisation of family visiting privileges for hospitalised children.

Bowlby developed Attachment Theory. He believed that an infant attachment was primarily a process of "proximity seeking" by the infant to an identified attachment figure in situations of stress and fear, in order to survive. "So long as the required proximity to the attachment figure can be maintained, no unpleasant feeling is experienced" (Bowlby 1969). This attachment is usually to the mother, but the child is able to attach to a constant caregiver of either sex who is responsive and sensitive to the child. This attachment happens between the child and the caregiver when the child is aged between 6 months and 2 years old.

Caregiver responses lead to the development of patterns of attachment; these in turn lead to "internal working models" which will guide the individual's feelings, thoughts and expectations in later relationships and give them confidence to venture out into the social world. Without such a secure relationship, the infant's normal social and emotional development will be severely impaired.

Bowlby believed that the behaviour shown by young children towards their parents would relate to the social behaviour the child would demonstrate in later life, and would affect how they functioned in future relationships.

> It is possible to predict future problems as early as 6 to 10 months of age, but not from the baby's temperament so much as from the mother's behaviour coupled with the baby's temperament. Mothers who are not "contingently" responsive to their baby's communications, who are not able to meet the needs of their particular baby and who impose their own goals on the baby, are likely to be helping to incubate future aggression and conduct disorders.
>
> (Gerhardt 2004)

Attachment Theory is relevant to the premise of this book, which is about recognising the source of the child's barriers to learning and making sense of the need for professionals to adapt their work practice to whom they are working with; and it is about their willingly forgoing the one-size-fits-all model.

Signalling

We are born with an inherited tendency to seek social stimulus and to form strong attachments to parents or caregivers. We also have a built-in tendency to detect and attend to human speech sounds, and we can recognise the smell of our mother. We are, physically, utterly dependent upon our mother or carer for our survival and well-being. We need to be able to bring our prime caregiver to us when we need them. Of course this is before we have language of any kind, so the first communication of our need is accomplished through signals.

> We signal to bring our mother to us through crying, smiling and babbling. The most effective signal is crying as the mother tends to come to her baby to check it is not in pain or hungry and the child gets the proximity of the prime care giver it needs. Smiling strengthens the attachment of the mother to the child as it elicits pleasure and she will often smile back, stroke, pat and talk to the child.
>
> (Bowlby 1969)

As the baby responds to its environment, connections are made in the brain by groups of neurons. These neurons react to repeated experiences and begin to shape pathways in the brain. We are all born with this raw potential from which the pathways of our expectations are made.

Expectations

The mother who always wakes her 1-year-old toddler in the morning with soft words and a cuddle, who lovingly bathes and dresses them, gently brushing their hair, is creating a pattern of experience that will structure the child's brain to expect this behaviour. The toddler in this world of nurture, love and kindness will begin to structure their brain to believe they are cared for and that the experience of touch and being looked after is pleasurable. If a child has a negative or painful experience of caregiving, if caregiving is frightening or neglectful, the child's expectations of caregiving and of adults in the future will be equally frightening and painful.

Our behaviour and our expectations from life are shaped through our experience of our parents and our environment. Our brain shapes who we are through repeated experience and stimuli. This repetition of experience will strengthen certain pathways, and "prune" others. We reflect the behaviour and manner of our being parented in our behaviour and expectations. If we are fed, held and cared for, we will thrive. If our level of care and interaction with our mother or prime carer is lacking, we will not thrive physically and our emotional and social development may be severely impaired.

An experiment was undertaken with a group of babies in which their foster-mothers were told to bathe and wash them, but not to "prattle" to them or speak to them. The conductor of the experiment wanted to see whether the babies would speak in the oldest known language, Hebrew, or if they would speak Greek, Latin or Arabic, or perhaps the language of their birth parents. They never spoke any language, because all the babies died. "They could not live without the petting and joyful faces and loving words of their foster mothers." This experiment was conducted by Fredrick II, Emperor of the Holy Roman Empire, in the thirteenth century (Provence and Lipton 1976).

The fact is that Maslow's Hierarchy of Needs has evolved into current educational thinking through the *Every Child Matters* agenda, and particularly into emotional health and well-being, identified 700 years ago through the work of the Emperor Frederick.

Social referencing

As time progresses and the toddler moves away from the secure base of its prime caregivers it will check back to its parent's face for cues on how to behave. The baby will begin to understand the signals of the mother; the attachment figure becomes the source of the child's social learning (Gerhardt 2004). The child's behaviour in checking to make sure its actions are safe is termed "social referencing". You will notice this behaviour in the classroom when children look at you to check if their action is safe or allowed. You are the prime carer and their point of safety. It is a behaviour we can recognise in ourselves, too, in situations when we are not sure what is the safe or correct action to take.

Attunement and reintegrative shame

In a secure attachment the baby becomes attuned to the mother, who is building a relationship to the outside world for the child. The child is beginning to learn how to explore its world. When a child explores something that is potentially unsafe, the mother will halt the child's exploration and the toddler will react by showing shame – usually by lowering the head or hiding the face and thereby

15

breaking the link between them. The toddler experiences shame, which checks the impulse to do the dangerous action. Most parents have experienced this when a toddler has gone to touch a hot plate or pick up a sharp object – the parent shouts "No!", the toddler is shocked, withdraws, and looks away and/or cries. The parent then comforts the toddler and explains that their action or impulse was dangerous; this re-establishes and reaffirms the attunement, and the child responds. The shame is reintegrated into the attunement, and the relationship and the secure base provided by the mother remains strong and secure. This pattern is called "reintegrative shame" (Braithwaite 1989).

This process is essential for impulse control and regulation; without it the child will not learn to regulate itself and its impulses to act. The same process regulates stress. The mother is teaching the child how to behave; by breaking the attunement she signals that the action or behaviour is not allowed, after which she reaffirms the attunement/relationship and the sense of safety. The formation of impulse control through reintegrative shame begins at around 9 months and continues until the child is about 18 months old. The child learns to regulate its impulses and is unlikely to repeat the action, because the feeling of shame when attunement is broken is uncomfortable. Other "affect" feelings such as surprise, interest and joy are nicer to experience. The shame feeling or "affect" is essential to the child in learning to regulate stress and impulse and to keep safe.

Disintegrative shame

When the child is continually shamed, shown contempt or rejected by its parent, and reaffirmation of attunement does not take place, the child is overwhelmed by "disintegrative shame", which gives rise to a range of disorders of thought, feeling and social functioning (Cairns 2002).

You may have seen the behaviour of a parent or caregiver who continually shouts at or derides their child as a matter of course. It becomes the mainstay of their relationship; there might be cuddles and comfort, but these are ephemeral and not the constant pattern or expectation of the child's experience of life. The continuous shame affect without the following attunement is disastrous for the child, who does not "attach", or develops "disorganised attachment"[6] to its parent. This shame can also develop into rage, as the child is overwhelmed by its unmet attachment needs. The child will not be able to regulate its impulses or behaviour. It will have an extremely negative view of itself, perceiving itself to be horrible or worthless. It finds it impossible to take compliments or to allow itself to succeed.

> [W]henever our daughter did well at school (and they worked very hard to help her achieve at her level and in her own quirky way), if she got a certificate for doing something, which she would never stand up and take in assembly, and we celebrated the event at home with a cake or a present, there would always be a kick-back. She would destroy the certificate, destroy her books or break the present that we had given her. She found it so hard to accept

any kind of positive success and feedback, it took her years to get a merit at secondary school and actually wear the badge for a day.

Interview with an adoptive parent (2009)

It is most likely that disintegrative shame will affect the well-being and behaviour of some of the children in your classroom, and you will need to think about your behaviour strategies for coping with them. Punitive measures, however light they may be, that continue this pattern of shame may reinforce the expectations these children have of being rejected by adults. Yet their expectation that you will reject them will be firmly planted; in fact, they may be working to get you to fulfil the expectations they have of adults.[7]

It is the strength of the confidence built by the child's early attachment figures that helps the child feel secure and be able to explore the wider world. This confidence to feel safe away from the mother is critical to the child's confidence in the school environment. It allows the child to transfer this positivity from home to nursery and to the challenging environment of school. Their attachment to and trust of their prime caregiver provides a model for them to trust their teacher. When a Reception class teacher was asked about the issues she faced in the classroom and her level of success with the children in making her pupils feel secure, she replied, "I always know I've cracked it when they call me 'mum' by mistake. For some of them it's a giggle, but for others it's a genuine desire to see me in that role" (Hawkins 2010).

It is not an uncommon occurrence for children to substitute the teacher in the parental role. The teacher becomes the child's point of safety in the classroom and, dependent upon the style of the head teacher, their safe person in the school. The teacher knows and nurtures the child, and has control of the teaching assistant, who may assume the role of the secondary parent in the child's mind. They are in their classroom family, but with a large number of siblings. So your role as teacher is to continue the teaching which the parent has taken on, knowingly or unknowingly, since they first held, cooed at and mirrored their baby's expressions back to them. This social learning never stops; we are practising and perfecting our social interplay with each other throughout our lives. We do not suddenly move into academic learning and stop developing our social skills – they are essential to our ability to be happy, to make and sustain relationships and to gain and sustain employment. We are not only teaching the social aspects of learning in our planned lessons; we are teaching them in our interactions with each other and with the children, every minute of our teaching day.

Regulation

Babies learn to regulate themselves by coordinating their systems with those of the adults around them. A baby does not have the mental capacity to regulate its feelings of comfort or distress but relies on its carers to soothe and comfort it, feed it when it is hungry and crying, and change it when it is soiled. The parent is sensitive to the baby's signals and restores the baby to a sense of comfort and well-being. As the baby grows, it becomes more aware of these feelings and, with the aid of the parent, can see that there are degrees of feeling angry or happy and begins to understand the range of feelings or emotions it is experiencing.

We see how crucial the parent–child relationship is in the context of the babies of depressed mothers who do not interact with them and give them only a low level of eye contact and care. These babies will adjust to low stimulation and become used to a lack of positive feelings, and they will develop a depressed way of interacting with other people (Gerhardt 2004). We learn to regulate our feelings and our behaviour through our experience of being parented.

The parent needs to be sufficiently mature, sensitive, caring and calm to regulate and contain our anxieties. How do we re-create, continue and develop this in the classroom environment and through our behaviour? We must think of the school as a home, and ourselves as carers who are continuing to support and strengthen the child as a social entity. We are teaching these social skills through our behaviour and our responses to their behaviour. We are regulating their behaviour through the way we listen and speak to them, and how we help them to understand and react to our signals. We are teaching them to understand their feelings and the feelings of others, encouraging the essential social skill of empathy. Without this, there cannot be emotional intelligence, because if we are unable to empathise we cannot share in, help with or understand the feelings of others.

We are teaching these skills (regulation, stress control and empathy) at the same time as we are teaching the curriculum; the two should be inextricably combined in our delivery of the learning experience. This is done through our demeanour, the environment we create in our classroom and the techniques we use for our delivery of the learning. Key to this are:

SAFE ENVIRONMENT: Make sure you know the adults who come into the room, and introduce anybody who comes into your space. Always tell the children the plan of the day in the morning so they know what will be happening (even if they cannot remember, they will feel that there is nothing to worry about – no surprises). In Reception and Year 1 make it clear that you will have toilet breaks, playtimes and lunch, and that they will be going home at the end of the school day.

SAFE, CALM, CONSISTENT ADULTS: Adults can help to regulate children's anxiety levels through their behaviour. Smiling in the morning as you greet the children and take the register is important; the first five minutes of your day can set the mood and tone for the next six hours. Your demeanour will be reflected back to you by the children. It is important to be consistent in your demeanour, your boundaries, your rules and your behaviour. Inconsistency confuses children and creates a feeling of unsafeness.

PERSONAL AREA: A child's peg, desk and place are very important, as they reflect the importance you and the school give to the child. The child should be encouraged to keep their area nice. It is very positive to have a drawer which they can perceive as their personal space (even in the self-care chaos that Reception can be!). Even a small area can become a centre of safety for a child.

Children who come from chaotic homes, where they are not given a sense of safety or a strong identity, can respond very well to a special area for their own possessions; the respect that must be given to this area will be part of the social skills learning of the class.

CLEAR ROUTINES: Build routines so that there is an order to the day. Make your own special class routines as well as embracing the routines of school life. Chaotic home environments will not pattern routine into a child's mind, and some children who have memory or processing difficulties will need help to remember what is happening during the day. You can help them to cope with the day by the routines and "rituals" you put into place. You can get the children to help with this by making charts, pictures and signs that will help them to own and know what different days will bring.

RULES AND BOUNDARIES: There need to be clear rules and boundaries for social interactions and behaviour in your class. You can set your own, or negotiate acceptable and unacceptable behaviours with the children. However you put these in place, you should try to give the children ownership and understanding of why they are there – "These rules keep us physically safe" or "These rules mean we can have a good time in class because you know what I expect from you". They can be tailor-made to help you regulate physical and emotional behaviour.[8]

JOY: There needs to be joy in the learning experience. Children should feel safe and sufficiently at ease to laugh with you and enjoy what you are teaching them. You should create a sense of fun, experimentation and achievement that is set at the level of the child's capabilities. It is interesting that children will not laugh when they do not feel safe and relaxed. The amount of laughter and joy in your classroom should be one of the ways you measure your success as a teacher.

What these behaviours are "saying" to the child:

- *Safe environment:* You will be safe and cared for in this classroom. I, the teacher, will make it safe for you and show you how to remain safe in it.
- *Safe, calm, consistent adults:* I will keep you safe. I can help you control and contain your anxiety and stress. I am the adult, I am in control of myself and the classroom.
- *Personal area:* You are important here, we respect and value you and make space for you. You have a safe place here for the things you care about and the things you use to learn. Learning is important.
- *Clear routines:* You are important. I will tell you what will happen. Nothing bad is going to happen. You know what you need to do next.
- *Rules and boundaries:* Rules keep us all safe. They are important and they have a purpose. You know the behaviour we want from you. We expect you to help us keep you safe. We expect you to help keep each other safe.

We expect certain behaviours of you. You are important enough to make the rules. You are responsible enough to keep them.

- *Joy:* You can be happy when you learn. In this "family" we trust each other enough to laugh and enjoy what we do. Learning can be fun and joyful. You enjoy yourself when you learn. Life and other people can be fun. We are having a nice time in school. We are in a happy class.

You will see from the above that we are putting elements from Maslow's Hierarchy into practical use: safety needs, belonging needs and the need for self-esteem. These should be built into all aspects of your delivery. You might be using them instinctively, but you need to identify where they sit in your delivery, and utilise and develop them.

Everything you put in place within the school and classroom will have a meaning to the children in your care. Just as, in the home environment, the level of care and comfort, and the parents' interest and engagement with their child, have a huge effect on the child's perception of itself, so too does the school environment and the teacher's connection with the pupil.

Each child sees its teacher through a separate pair of eyes, and from a different set of experiences. The teacher might perceive their class as thirty separate individuals, or as a corporate group. Each child sees its teacher as a powerful figure. This can have an immense effect upon the child's emotional and academic life. This is dependent on the degree to which the child connects with or attaches to the teacher. Some teachers connect more with some children than with others. Is this because the child and the teacher become "attuned" to each other? We might not acknowledge that we have "favourites" in our class, but this will happen; it is part of human nature. The teacher must balance a feeling of dislike or non-connection with a child with the need to connect the child with the learning and with itself. Children with challenging behaviours can be difficult to like. They may be working hard to make you not like them, so as to confirm their feelings of worthlessness.

For some teachers the concept of being *in loco parentis* is an accepted part of their self-perception in the classroom. In a Reception class, one might be more open to the ethos of the teacher who "parents" as well as teaches, because the children are young and moving from their parents' care into yours – they are perceived by society as being vulnerable and needy. We respond to little ones in a caring, protective way; we understand their need to attach to us.

Year 5 and Year 6 teachers may not perceive themselves in this light, but rather as mentors who are preparing the child for transition to secondary school and giving them the self-reliance that is required in that environment. Yet the relationship between the child and the teacher is crucial at all stages of the child's personal and academic development. The teacher is a conduit through which to channel learning. The child feels safe with the teacher, connects with them; and through this connection the teacher engages with the child to experience the learning. The child who is nurtured in its home environment and has been given a secure base will still require the teacher to give it access to the learning.

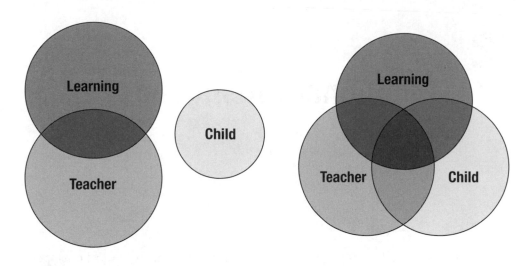

FIGURE 1.3 Child not attaching to the teacher   **FIGURE 1.4** Child attaching to the teacher

This child will find connecting in a positive way easier, as it is a natural part of its expectation of life.

The more vulnerable child may have greater difficulty in attaching to the teacher. It may exhibit challenging behaviour because it doesn't feel safe or it is angry and anxious. The first steps to controlling and easing this behaviour are taken through the behaviour of the teacher. The trust between child and teacher will grow, and become a model for other social relationships for the child. It can reaffirm the positive attachment and relationships a child has forged with adults, and it can help model a positive relationship for a child who has a more vulnerable background. It can help the child to build trust and respect for adults.

Bowlby's theory of attachment has long been the bedrock of the theory and practice of social work. It is time for the theory and practical teaching in the primary school to take a proper account of it as well.

Bowlby states that well–based self-reliance "is usually the product of slow and unchecked growth from infancy into maturity during which, through interaction with trustworthy and encouraging others, a person learns how to combine trust in others with trust in himself" (Bowlby 1989).

You have the opportunity to make a huge impact upon the children in your care. In the school environment, you are Bowlby's "encouraging other".

2

Emotional Intelligence

Emotions are things that happen to us rather than things we make happen. We try to manipulate our emotions all the time but all we are doing is rearranging the outside world to trigger certain emotions — we cannot control our reactions directly [. . . .] The wiring of the brain favours emotion.

(Carter 1999)

EMOTION: Comes from the Latin *mōtus* meaning movement. Our emotions are always moving in us; we respond to everything we see and hear emotionally, and then we reason. When you face your new class you will have an emotional response to them before your reasoned one emerges. When you are faced with a behavioural problem your first response will be emotional, and then you will reason what your coping strategy will be.

Our emotions protect us. The reason we have an instant emotional response to situations is to keep us safe. As animals, we are primed to assess our environment for predators or dangers, and this facility is heightened when we are in unsafe circumstances. The safety stage in Maslow's Hierarchy is about feeling secure, knowing that the environment we inhabit holds no threats.

When we are confident and are faced with a new environment, a new person or a new experience, our first response will be "Do I like him/her/it?"

We have patterned expectations, responses and behaviours that have developed in us from the age of 6 months through our experience of being parented.

It is necessary to understand how our emotional receptors develop when we are talking about emotional intelligence and trying to understand what it is and how we, as educators, can facilitate a greater understanding and experience of emotional intelligence in the children whom we teach, and the importance and effectiveness of experiential learning. We have talked about how the brain develops expectations of life through the repeated stimuli we receive as babies. Our understanding of emotions is also shaped by our intimate relationship with our prime carer.

AFFECT: Refers to the experience of feeling or emotion. Affect display is facial, gestural or vocal behaviour. When we are babies our parents reflect our emotions and feelings back to us by their facial expressions and tones: as our mother holds us we smile, she smiles and shows pleasure, we smile more, she talks to us and holds us for a longer time. As we develop these expressions our parents reflect or mirror them back to us, and we realise that they are "showing" us our feelings. Eventually this allows us to interpret both our own and others' feelings and thoughts. Our parents identify our feelings for us and label them. Usually this happens unselfconsciously (Gerhardt 2004). When we have experienced and learnt these expressions, we can read them in the physicality and vocal tones of those around us. This is affect display, a skill we continue to use throughout our lives in our social and emotional dealings with each other. The child who has not experienced this process in its development will not read the signals of pleasure or displeasure in the teachers and children around them.

COGNITION: (Latin: *cognoscere*, meaning "to know" or "to recognise") Cognition is the scientific term for "the process of thought" to knowing. In a simplistic sense the cognitive part of the brain is where the reasoning and processing of knowledge takes place.

CONATION: (Latin: *conatus*, meaning inclination or impulse) Conation might be defined as impulse. The conative part of the mind takes emotional feelings and thoughts/knowledge and directs how you act upon them.

The affective part of the mind deals with emotions, the cognitive part reasons or processes the emotions, and the conative part motivates action or behaviour.

    Affect
    Behaviour
    Cognition

We learn how emotions are expressed by others and by ourselves; we learn how to reason, understand and regulate our emotions; then we act on what we have learnt and respond; this is our behaviour.

These divisions have been referred to as the "ABC of psychology".

When a child has not learnt about affect and how emotions are expressed, it will not be able to recognise or read social signals. If facial signals are not understood, that is when a child's responses will perplex, aggravate and challenge the teacher or a classmate. You may be signalling to a noisy child to be quiet by a nod or a disapproving eye and fixed mouth, but the child goes on chatting, or humming to itself. When other children are being sensitive to your signals in the classroom and regulating their behaviour accordingly, it will seem that the child who ignores these signals is wilfully misbehaving. This can undermine your confidence in your class's perception of your control, but you must see it in the context of the child's behaviour and not your own. If the child cannot

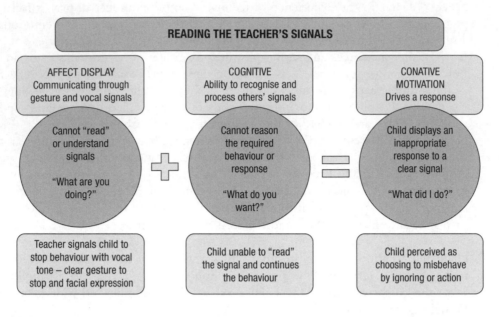

FIGURE 2.1 Reading the teacher's signals

read signals, it is not choosing to ignore you, it simply does not understand. Your signalling is like a foreign language the child was never taught.

Empathy requires the ability to understand and imaginatively enter the feelings of another person, so as to make sense of the messages transmitted by the behaviour of that person. We must remember that empathy is a cognitive skill. We are not born with the capacity to understand the emotions and feelings of our parents and the people around us. We learn to do this through attachment, attunement, social referencing and affect.

Children who cannot process information easily cannot be empathetic. The faces and behaviours of others do not make sense. Traumatised children are also preoccupied and burdened, so they have little motivation to be in touch with the experience of others. Their own experience is exhausting enough (Cairns and Stanway 2004).

As part of SEAL delivery, teachers are asked to show children photographs, images, or to circle faces that look "sad" or "happy". Children with a lack of affect may not understand what a picture of a child's unhappy face is meant to transmit to them. Responding to questions in an interview, a teacher said that a particular child could not say what emotion the photo of another child's very obviously unhappy face signified. He could not read the emotion in the expression (Hawkins 2010).

> Socially rejected children typically are poor at reading emotional and social signals and when they do read such signals, they may have a limited repertoire for response.
>
> (Golman 1996)

A photograph or a picture is also separate from the living experience of a moving, animated face. The teacher will need to show and explain the expression and ask the child to mimic or mirror it:

> This is my happy face. When I have a happy feeling in my tummy because something nice has happened, I smile like this. [*teacher models the face*] Now show me your happy face, think of something nice [. . .] does it make you want to smile? [*teacher models the smile*]

The teacher continues to model the face of the emotion to the child, and when the child mirrors it, the teacher reflects it back to the child.

Next, the teacher tries to connect the emotion to the expression. This example of teaching or reaffirming of affect is occurring far later in the child's development than it should (as we have seen, it would usually be taught in infancy by the prime carer), but it may help build the child's understanding of the language by which feelings are communicated through facial expressions. The Feeling Cards exercises described in Part 7 have been shaped to support this work of teaching feelings and emotional signals.

There will be children, therefore, who are not *choosing* to disobey your signals in the classroom, or to not understand that they are upsetting the other children. They are simply not conditioned to read the social and emotional signals that are coming their way. Children who have suffered severe parental neglect will often present inappropriate social behaviours, cuddling teachers and adults whom they don't know, or invading other children's space by getting too close to them. This can be misinterpreted as confrontational behaviour, but the child will not read the signals telling them to give space and pull back. This inappropriate behaviour comes from a background in which the child has not been taught the absolute basics of social behaviour – the reading of emotional and social signals; they find it extremely difficult to interpret their own or others' emotions.

If, as teachers, we labour under the misapprehension that we are born with empathy, we might consequently find it very difficult to deal with a challenging non-empathetic child. It is possible that this non-empathetic child has not learned how to relate to the feelings of other children. Understanding this can be a great help when forming strategies to help change the behaviour. Believing that we are born with empathy is a common mistake when our understanding of others seems like second nature to us – in fact our understanding *is* second nature, since it comes only once we are taught it.

It is here that the school can act as the constant safe, trusted family, by providing the child who has not had a positive secure base with a role model of what life can provide, holding them with care in a safe environment, with structures, routines and positive adult role models. The school can teach a child interpersonal and intrapersonal skills, giving it access to understanding and managing emotions, learning self-regulation and social skills, so that it can achieve its greatest learning success – the path to empathy, learning and self-esteem.

The emotionally intelligent school

> We know too much and feel too little. At least, we feel too little of those creative emotions from which a good life springs.
>
> Bertrand Russell[1]

> The behaviour in school of the large majority of children is good, as it always has been. Where instances of bad behaviour occur intervention must be swift, intelligent and effective. This intervention must protect the interests of the majority while aiming to change the behaviour of those causing the difficulties.
>
> (Steer 2009)

The Behaviour Challenge reflects a key recommendation of Sir Alan Steer's final report on behaviour standards and practices in schools (*Learning Behaviour: Lessons Learned*) in which he made clear that an Ofsted judgement of "satisfactory" with regard to behaviour should be seen as "not good enough" and should trigger additional support.[2]

It also takes forward the commitments, in the *21st Century Schools* White Paper, on the pupil guarantee that every child should be able to go to a school where there is good behaviour, strong discipline, order and safety; and the parent guarantee about ensuring that parents fulfil their responsibilities for pupil behaviour.

It is interesting to compare the findings and recommendations housed within the Behaviour Challenge set by Steer following a number of previous reports. A practising headteacher, Steer was commissioned by the Secretary of State for Education to undertake a comprehensive survey, and subsequently to author five substantial reports over a period of several years on the current state of play within schools across the country with regard to the issue of pupil behaviour, how it was being addressed and managed. It is very pertinent that Steer, in line with the philosophy of this book, reinforces the inextricable link between good teaching and good behaviour. In "Delivering the Behaviour Challenge", Steer writes:

> Good behaviour and strong discipline go hand in hand with effective teaching and learning. Teachers cannot teach effectively and pupils cannot learn effectively in classes disrupted by poor behaviour ... By the same token, excellent teaching that engages pupils can reduce the likelihood that disruptive behaviour will occur.
>
> (Steer 2009)

The key then, according to Steer, is the level of teaching standards and pedagogy within the school for both teaching and non-teaching staff.

Some questions that might be posed to assess standards of teaching and levels of pedagogy within a particular school are as follows:

- How would you describe relationships: (1) between children and staff; (2) between children; and (3) between staff?

- How would you describe the approach to teaching within the school?
- How would you describe the approach to learning within the school?
- Who is responsible for the teaching and learning in school?
- What are the priorities of the school?
- What part does respect play in the running of the school?
- How does the school prepare the child to be resilient?
- How does the school describe itself?
- In what ways would you say the school is particularly effective?
- Does the school recognise its shortcomings and (if there are shortcomings) how is it going about dealing with them?

These questions relate to the emotional maturity of the school. The answers will depend upon the current ethos of the school, which in turn will inevitably depend upon where the school stands in relation to its effectiveness in serving the needs of the education community. The ethos is inevitably organic and will flicker and fluctuate. The resolve remains. As Mahatma Ghandi said: "You must be the change you want to see in the world" (quoted in Killick 2006).

Killick continues by stating that it is only through teachers working together and with others who share an interest in this area that change occurs: "We best help children develop emotional literacy by developing it in ourselves."

How then do we directly challenge and confront the need to change and update the culture/ethos within our school?

As teachers we are shaped by our surroundings and by the environment within which we work, but we also have the power to change things, our pupils and ultimately ourselves. If there is a problem for an individual teacher within a particular school (for example, among the staff, or indeed with the direction in which the school is perceived to be heading), how can change be brought about? It is a fact that acceptance of the status quo, or indeed criticism of it when tempered by a lack of motivation to make change, can seriously damage our children.

What are the pressures placed upon teachers that can prevent them from making change, particularly beyond their training? There are those who complain of being hijacked out of the classroom, who change and who subsequently compromise their beliefs and the very factors which brought them into the profession in the first place. Is it merely the issues of accountability, of maintaining or developing achievement within the school to satisfy statistics, and the hugely increased pressures of inspection and self-evaluation? Add to these the constant stream of initiatives from central government that make education the political football it has become. Are we being fair to expect teachers to adapt to these new initiatives and trends? How, in these circumstances, is it possible for us to feel empowered and strong enough to develop our individual emotional literacy to be able to cope with, manage and thrive on change?

The triangle of effective learning

Linking the triangle of emotional intelligence, behaviour and the positive use of positional drama in teaching approaches enhances the opportunity for effective learning. The practical application of the thinking of authors such as Bodine and Crawford (1999) is embodied in the teaching approach of positional drama. There is a positive and common "Construction of Reality" within this work which gives a context to the development of emotional intelligence. If one is to agree that the prerequisite for learning for all or children is the ability to be able to control and manage emotion in order to open the door to learning, Bodine and Crawford recognise the importance and wider relevance of this assumption by asserting that, with the support of the school, and by using appropriate teaching strategies, all young people can participate fully in society "through the exercise of responsible behavioural choices".

How can young people be given the opportunity to make informed choices? The answer is that they can do so only when presented with a focus for their learning. The practical application of this work comes under the heading of Positional Drama. This enables young people to engage at their own level and to experience at first hand the feeling of empowerment and self-awareness at a level potentially hitherto undiscovered within their academic career in school. This feeling or emotion is the trigger for many to learn.[3] It is the point of emotional engagement which provokes the opportunity for the most effective point of learning. If schools are to be supporting and enabling theatres of learning, there has to be a recognition and realisation amongst all responsible adults in the school community that preparedness and a positive view towards embracing a caring, dynamic and supportive environment is essential for optimum learning among all pupils. Bodine and Crawford (1999) continue: "Schools must be places where children feel valued, useful and needed." For some it may be the only place in their lives where they have the opportunity to be thus regarded, and therefore the responsibility on the school community to facilitate this is immense, and cannot be underestimated in terms of commitment and resolve and as a measure of school effectiveness.

If children do feel confident about their own feelings, and secure in their environment, they are more likely to be able to learn and develop their learning in an environment conducive to exploration and discovery, and the type and format of that learning is therefore crucial to measuring success. Positional Drama is a vehicle for transporting children into a learning zone that is safe and encourages experimentation, while securing an environment in which the individual is only as exposed as far as they wish.

Therefore it is essential that in facilitating children's paths into a specific way of working that enables them to discover and grow, positively encouraged by all those who work in the school community, a belief system regarding expectation and potential achievement must be shared among all members of that community.

Self-efficacy

Self-efficacy lies at the centre of this shared belief. It may be described as a belief we hold as to how far we will be able to achieve success in a particular area. To hold a belief that success for all can be achieved is a prerequisite for any development of a school towards offering a more enabling and supportive environment for all children. The environment can be developed to cope with all types of young people and may not always rely upon an institution that dictates without consultation, which by its very definition can exclude some children from the mainstream within the school.

There is a relationship between preparedness, classroom experience and self-efficacy as factors which may contribute to the development of confident teachers. Teachers who have had classroom experiences with behaviours that were tolerable and manageable develop a higher sense of self-efficacy in classroom management.

For developing an ethos within a school community that is both engaging and inclusive, the above has to apply. How staff can enhance their own work in terms of addressing their own practice and adapting it to suit the needs of all pupils is very complex. To place the emphasis on learning without trepidation is the key. Positional Drama is an embodiment of a resource available to all teachers, individually and collectively, as a tried-and-trusted approach to enable all pupils to work and to achieve alongside each other. A further reference to Bodine and Crawford (1999) relates directly to the work undertaken in the Positional Drama detailed later in the book, leading to "self-awareness, self-control, empathy, cooperation and constructive conflict resolution".

These aims are implicit in the practical case studies of teaching outlined later in the book. Indeed, it is appropriate to suggest that reaching these aims should surely be implicit in any teaching. The short response is that evidently it is not. As mentioned earlier, it is the context that is the most important factor in determining whether or not the above aims can be found consistently throughout the school community. This volume goes further, in that it applies the aims in the context of planning and classroom activities, thereby giving them credence and currency, in that all children can see the point within a constructed reality of being put in a situation whereby they are obliged to give a response. Their response, however, will have consequences for all involved, and will be a real responsibility for themselves and others that is only too rarely given to young people in the context of their everyday learning. It is the learning which can in turn allow children to alter, adapt and tailor their behaviour to suit the needs of the work in which they are involved in a clear, informed way, something that is frequently lacking in a whole school environment.

This is at the heart of what is becoming regarded as emotional intelligence. An emotionally literate school with emotionally literate children is an ideal, but one that is achievable. It is the realisation that an emotionally literate school can develop only as fast as the community can accept, and that for both teacher and pupil the common denominator is teaching and learning. No amount of government intervention can shape the classroom and the school corridors to place an emphasis upon teaching and learning which enables all pupils to grow as a community. The tools are in the planning, and in the ability of teaching and non-teaching staff to take protected risks. This refers to taking risks with their teaching methods, putting aside their tried-and-trusted teaching strategies and adopting strategies that might invite greater understanding of what can be achieved within their own subject area – effectively stepping out of their comfort zone in terms of their own pedagogy. When we are using an experiential form of learning, the content can become more relevant to the time in which we are living.

Change will need to take the form of discarding tired methods of teaching. This is not the time for a revolution in pedagogy; rather it is a time to cherry-pick good practice and take it into a new arena of pedagogy which overtly promotes the need to develop emotional literacy in children, and in all staff who come into contact with children within the community, to enable children to be engaged in their learning and realise their full potential. It is no longer appropriate to foster behaviour programmes of punitive intent and divorce those programmes from mainstream learning. It is time to look at the child who is disruptive as a learner, as one having potential, and as one for whom all staff have high expectations. The child will be a hurt child, and rather than cure it with punitive central behaviour strategies, it is time to embrace it within the mainstream and give it the tools to learn and the emotional intelligence to cope with learning. Initially the child will be asked to respond, take part, engage and subsequently assume responsibility for its behaviour and its learning in tandem, not in isolation. It is the child's role as a learner that will develop and enhance appropriate, emotionally intelligent behaviour. Too often the solution to behaviour issues has concentrated on modification through sanction and punishment, and now is the time to enable behaviour through the methodology of learning and consistent emotionally intelligent teaching within an emotionally intelligent education community.

As we have seen, the emotionally intelligent community has to be triggered by the initiative and vision of an emotionally intelligent leadership, one which recognises the importance of the work described later in this book. What is it, then, that leaders who are emotionally literate have to comprehend in order to provide for an emotionally literate education environment?

Brenda Beatty, addressing an education conference in Sydney in 2000, maintained that "People will forget what you said. People will forget what you did. But people will never forget how you made them feel." A good and lasting example of this is the number of people who remember the one or two teachers from their schooldays who had a major influence. More often than not, this was because those teachers made them feel good about themselves, believed in them, and gave them praise for an area of their work or contribution. It felt good at the time, and it has remained in their memory throughout childhood and adulthood.

Emotionally literate leadership

Emotionally literate leadership is characterised by Beatty (2000) as:

- Visionary leadership – to be shared by all within the community
- Principle-centred leadership – trust displayed by all at all levels

- Sapiential leadership – respected for good practice prior to taking up a position of leadership

- Shared leadership – understanding of followership[4] and subsequent delegation of responsibility.

John MacBeath (MacBeath and Mortimore 2001) refers to the many forms of leadership appropriate to the particular situation in which one finds oneself and remarks that "Leadership is a term full of ambiguity and a range of inter-pretations. It is a humpty dumpty word that can mean, just what we want it to mean." MacBeath believes it is good, emotionally, that literacy will enable the leadership to respond and adapt to changing circumstances within the organisation.

It is perhaps appropriate here to recognise the relationship between emotionally literate leadership and the impact of the work being described within this book. One is a prerequisite for the other. Too often it has been suggested in schools that the key to the success of a particular project is consistency. It is true to say that, in the case of emotionally literate education, community work on developing emotionally literate children cannot be sustained without the agreement and support of all. Only when the approach by all to the children is consistent, and we allow children to achieve, thrive and succeed no matter what their academic ability, will the pedagogical dilemma be solved.

Part of this process towards achieving an emotionally literate community in which children thrive is the need to equip them and indeed the staff with a healthy degree of resilience. Resilient children, working with emotionally intelligent staff, can develop:

- Positive peer and adult interactions
- A positive sense of self
- A sense of personal power rather than powerlessness
- An internal locus of control.

A resilient child, according to Winfield (1994), is one who possesses "the relative strength of individual characteristics and external protective processes compared to the influence of risks and vulnerabilities in the external environment".

A pedagogical dilemma!

Howard Gardner

The name Howard Gardner is established as being synonymous with the concept of "Multiple Intelligences". Gardner has been publishing work around the concept of intelligence and creativity since 1973, and published a major work on intelligence in 1993 (Gardner 1993). It is worth mentioning, before we examine the impact of Gardner's work on the construction of this book, that Gardner has worked against the constant backdrop of acceptance of the notion of the all-embracing "Intelligent Person", personified by the work of Hernstein and Murray (1994). For the purpose of this book, a consideration of the contrasting views on the concept of intelligence is essential if we are to pinpoint the relevance of the theory of intelligence before establishing what is meant by the emotionally intelligent school.

Hernstein and Murray state that "Intelligence is best thought of as a single property distributed within the general population along a bell shaped curve". Some of their findings were that:

- Comparatively few people have very high intelligence (IQ over 130)
- Comparatively few people have very low intelligence (IQ under 70)
- Most people are clumped together (IQ 85–115)
- Intelligence is hereditary.

They concluded that many of our current social ills are due to the behaviour and capacity of people with relatively low intelligence. Evidence shows that those with low intelligence are more likely to be on benefits, involved in crime, come from broken homes, drop out of school and so on.

Hernstein's views have been endorsed by some psychologists who specialise in measurement, and the reader is driven to the conclusion that the number of unintelligent people must be reduced.

In contrast, Howard Gardner states that:

> Intelligence itself is not a content, but is geared to specific contents. E.g. linguistic intelligence is activated when people encounter the sounds of language or when they wish to communicate something verbally to others [. . . .] Intelligences should be mobilized to help people learn important content and not used as a way of categorizing individuals.
>
> (Gardner 1999)

Psychologist Robert Sternberg defines human intelligence as "mental activity directed toward purposive adaptation to, selection and shaping of, real-world environments relevant to one's life" (Sternberg 1985), which means that intelligence is how well an individual deals with environmental changes throughout their lifespan. Sternberg's "triarchic" model of intelligence comprises three parts: componential, experiential and practical.

He maintains that same components will operate whatever the kind of material is being processed. Sternberg's work became very important to psychologists. He identified that intelligences do not have to operate independently, and there may well be an overlap – for example, between mathematics and music. He further maintained that there is no single unit of memory-like intelligence; that no separate artistic intelligence exists; and that all intelligences function artistically or non-artistically. Multiple intelligence ideas have grown comfortably in schools that highlight the arts, uncomfortably in schools where the arts have been marginalised.

It is relevant to this argument to ask the question: Do schools with multiple intelligence focus work?

According to Mindy Kornhaber (Gardner *et al.* 1996), in a study of forty-one schools applying MI theory for at least three years:

- 78 per cent of schools reported positive standardised test outcomes
- 63 per cent attributed improvement to practices inspired by MI theory
- 78 per cent reported improved performances by students with learning difficulties
- 81 per cent reported improvement in parent participation
- 81 per cent reported improved student discipline
- 67 per cent attributed these results to MI theory.

There is a stark contrast between the opposing theories of Gardner and Hernstein. Hernstein and Murray's (1994) assertion in *The Bell Curve* was that social pathology is due to low intelligence and that intelligence cannot be significantly changed through social interaction.

If we are to accept this assertion, it is the role of the education community to find a way of reducing the number of unintelligent people. There is potentially something quite sinister about this view. The majority response to *The Bell Curve* was very negative, except from the politically conservative ranks. Gardner maintains that its publication was deliberately kept under wraps until after the book was reviewed by sympathetic educationalists. At about the same time that *The Bell Curve* and Gardner's own *Intelligence Reframed* came out, Golman's *Emotional Intelligence* (1996) was published and was warmly greeted by Gardner. He praised it for highlighting the importance of working with others, of empathy and understanding of others' emotions, and the recognition of their feelings.

In contrast to the theory of intelligence commonly held by Hernstein among others, Gardner defined intelligence in 1983 as "Having the ability to solve problems or create products that are valued within one or more cultural settings". By 1999, in *Intelligence Reframed*, he had refined his definition to "the bio-psychological potential to process information that can be activated in a cultural setting, to solve problems or create products that are of value in a culture".

For teaching children and making sense of our pedagogy, the work of Gardner is extremely defining. It takes the teacher away from the assumption that intelligence can only be measured through linguistic and numerical competency. The fact that Gardner equates kinaesthetic intelligence, interpersonal and intra-personal, alongside word and number, removes the rather negative view of assessing a young person's ability within such tight parameters as the linguistic and mathematical. The seven intelligences should become the key to successful learning and celebration for a large number of children who up until that point may have known nothing but failure in their school career. Gardner refers to the assessment tools utilised to accurately assess a child's level of intelligence in one or more areas in the early years and allow the results to influence the planning of the teacher and the types of activity most suited to the individual.

The "spectrum classroom allows assessment of pupils utilising materials which represent fully the seven intelligences and decisions made on the form of curriculum most suited emanate from the spectrum". Gardner adheres very much to the notion of "individually configured education".

The education community is currently working on the journey towards personal education and the individual timetable. It is interesting that children with barriers to their learning and those who may find themselves in alternative education are supported with Individual Education Plans, or Personal Learning Plans, and latterly Information Passports, which list strengths, background, interests, performance, anxiety, experience and goals. The curriculum is then adapted to suit such requirements. Why is it that we cannot provide for all children using these plans?

The alternative curriculum arrived at through the process of assessment of the seven intelligences will, according to Gardner, still contain a common core. There will still be a section on the history of your country, basic laws and the definition of algebra and geometry. The key is very much about a personalised, constructed curriculum, relevant and pertinent to an individual's type of intelligence(s), but highlighted as the key to learning for that child.

> Being committed to success for all members of the community, rather than success for some at the expense of others. That's why norm-referencing is such a dangerous fellow-traveller for all schools, where we have a moral duty to treat children as they might become, rather than as they infuriatingly are.
>
> (Brighouse 2006)

Self-efficacy is a belief we hold as to how far we will be able to achieve success in a particular area. First and foremost it behoves the teacher/pupil–school/parent to share a belief that success can be achieved. Without this, the notion of achievement may either be one-way or non-existent, ensuring failure and disappointment. So how can we be assured that there is a shared belief in the positivity of success?

Teachers most effective in dealing with challenging behaviour are those who are most confident in their ability to teach difficult students. Teachers high in self-efficacy are more likely to use positive teaching strategies, such as praise, modifying teaching and differentiation. The self-efficacy levels of practising teachers with greater than six years' experience improved, but not to pre-service levels.

What are the factors, if they exist, which may be present in changing approaches and encouragement for effort? Levels of self-efficacy as teachers enter into full-time teaching: how might they be avoided? The feeling of preparedness is essential in the development of confidence in one's ability to execute a certain behaviour. Teachers who have classroom experiences with behaviours that were tolerable and manageable develop a higher sense of self-efficacy in classroom management. How in practice can teachers utilise a specific pedagogical approach to enhance their and their students' sense of self-efficacy and in turn create more consistently rich and rewarding experiences for the student? Some of the following individual teaching approaches will lay the foundation for this to occur.

First and foremost, pupils will need to feel that the teacher treats them fairly, and is committed to teaching them. Over time, the teacher will speak to each pupil individually about topics that interest them. To enhance self-belief (efficacy) the teacher will need to:

- Show concern that pupils should feel secure with their physical environment and emotionally engaged
- Use language in a way that builds relationships and raises pupils' self-esteem
- Establish classroom routines with which pupils are familiar
- Begin lessons by establishing at the outset what it is the teacher wants pupils to learn, and why
- Explain the lesson and how it will help pupils to learn better
- Welcome and be positive. Smile at all of them, even the ones whom the teacher finds difficult or uncooperative
- Engage class in the first minute with something about today's lesson or something from the last one
- Try to notice something positive about each pupil, and say their names when addressing them
- Identify expected learning outcomes using language with which the pupils can easily engage
- Be gently persistent and consistent
- Ask pupils to identify two or three key points they have learned from the lesson, working in pairs and recording in words or pictures
- Summarise the learning, reminding them of the context in terms of both previous and future lessons
- Set the scene for the following lesson
- Say goodbye and thank the pupils for a good lesson.

The language we use with our students is crucial to shared belief and to motivating young people: "I know you can" is challenging yet motivational; "You can do it. What help do you need?" is the language of hope; "I believe you can do this" is the language of belief.

The language of possibility

Students place limits on what they think is possible, believing a task is beyond their capability. Lack of self-belief affects their motivation and their commitment to learning. "I can't do this, it's boring" signals "I don't believe I can be successful with this and therefore I don't want to take the risk — it may or may not be boring." As teachers we should be able to shift our language to suit the situation.

Language should support learning; we need to remove the language of failure. We need to avoid telling students that they are wrong. Say "You are a step nearer", rather than "You're wrong again". Do not use blame language and avoid appearing to blame students for their lack of learning. Rather, ask, "Which bit haven't I explained enough?" Use positive words and phrases such as:

- When you finish [. . .]
- I know you can [. . .]
- Which part didn't I explain enough?
- I'm sorry, I should have made that clear [. . .]
- What do we need to remember here?
- Up until now this bit has proved a little tricky [. . .]
- Today you have a great opportunity [. . .]
- You will remember [. . .]
- It's your choice/you decide [. . .]

The passionate teacher

Addressing a local school conference to mark forty years of comprehensive education, Professor Tim Brighouse developed the ideal outlined in the previous section by referring to the teacher's need to differentiate approach rather than task. He talked of the important role to be played in the future by the "passionate teacher", whom he defined as one having "a fascination for the potential for growth in people, a depth and fervour about doing things and [one who strives] for excellence for all pupils".

In accepting many of Brighouse's assertions it is important in the current education arena to reconsider and revisit the role of the teacher, and the peda-gogical approaches available to the teacher in effectively dealing with challenging behaviour. The teacher is charged with developing and deepening the learning experience in the classroom for all pupils. It could be argued in the current educational climate that there is even more pressure on the individual teacher to "succeed" in terms of exam results and added value. Does this then minimise the impact of the passionate teacher and effectively dilute the potential for growth in all pupils? This book begins to address these issues from a stance of questioning whether the teacher in the current educational climate is allowed to develop and practise inclusive pedagogical approaches without having a detrimental effect upon the learning of others. Or does the teacher have to implement a punitive behaviour policy in order to maximise the success of a much smaller cohort of pupils at the "top end" in order to fulfil targets? If so, at what cost to the relation-ship between pupil and teacher?

The issue of classroom behaviour has been on the education agenda for the past thirty years. In 1998, the DfES introduced the notion of Social Inclusion

(DfES 1998). This document was intended to highlight the debate on educational inclusion which was a direct result of the 1994 UNESCO Salamanca Statement on the rights of all children across the world to a "fair and equitable education".

This book will examine the pervading sources of barriers to pupils' learning and to effecting a positive pedagogical response by examining the source of particular challenging behaviour. In practice it will be important to discover whether there are successful pedagogical approaches that might be adopted by teachers to counteract and deal effectively with challenging behaviour. Pedagogy in this context refers to the "art of teaching" and the potential power the teacher wields over the quality of learning within the classroom. Pedagogy refers to the limitless potential that teachers possess to shape learning to include all pupils and to retain high expectations for all, notwithstanding many of the barriers that pupils might erect in order to compromise their own ability to learn.

Pedagogy is also the art of enabling such pupils alongside other pupils who may not share those barriers. The connection between pedagogy and behaviour is based on the premise that it will become necessary to investigate teaching approaches, which will subsequently improve the learning environment for all pupils including those who display challenging behaviour. How far are we, as teachers, tolerant with our pupils? If we accept that tolerance of certain behaviours is variable depending upon the individual teacher, what teaching approaches can we employ to enhance and sharpen tolerance without being detrimental to the learning opportunities of the whole class? Fundamental to this work is the notion that schools can really absorb and utilise deviant behaviour in order to enhance the learning experience of all pupils, as opposed to the simple notion that in all cases the deviant behaviour has to be challenged, modified or removed.

> A disruptive child is always a hurt child. A disaffected, withdrawn child who seldom turns up to school is also a hurt child. Parents who cannot sort out these problems are parents who do not have the resources to carry out their job which, unlike teaching, is unpaid and never-ending. Where a school or LEA are committed to developing inclusive policies based on equality and compassion, they do not have to resort to punishing or rejecting troubled children, but find ways to help them instead.
>
> (Mason 1996)

Children with emotional and behavioural difficulties have special education needs, in that they have learning difficulties on account of the barriers that they face.

What makes a good teacher? A good teacher:

- Understands pupils and their needs
- Is one to whom pupils can relate, talk to and feel they won't be shown up
- Enjoys their subject
- Knows their subject but not so well that they think they are superior
- Has a sense of humour but knows when to stop

- Understands that some pupils don't "get it" straight away
- Sets standards at the start so that pupils know where they stand
- Has the willpower to treat all pupils the same
- Is a good listener
- Knows what is relevant to the course
- Takes an interest in the pupil as a person
- Is not sexist or racist
- Practices what they preach (e.g. marks work punctually).

The inclusive classroom

> The inclusive classroom one which with a continuing emphasis on individual differences leads all pupils, irrespective of social or cultural background, disability or difficulty in learning to succeed in terms of fulfilment of academic and social goals, and in the development of positive attitudes to self and others.
>
> (Alban–Metcalfe 2002)

Inclusive education is achieved by schools that are committed to maximising inclusion and minimising exclusion. They plan for diversity and work towards developing an appropriate environment for all pupils rather than obliging all pupils to fit the school. The premise is that effecting positive behaviour through positive learning experiences inverts the practice of establishing good behaviour in order for all pupils to learn.

This behaviour for learning approach pre-empts the notion that the key to successful learning for all pupils is to establish a punitive behaviour policy with rewards and punishments so as to maintain a purposeful learning environment.

> Bad behaviour in schools is a complex problem which does not lend itself to simple solutions.
>
> (Elton Report 1989)

The above statement is quoted directly from the report of the 1989 Committee of Enquiry under the chairmanship of Lord Elton. In 2005, a group of practitioners chaired by Sir Alan Steer was commissioned to identify good practice which promoted good behaviour and that might be "adopted by all schools". The report was published in two parts, in October 2005 and March 2006. The key issue emanating from this report was an echo of Elton's findings (Elton Report 1989) – the need to seek a more consistent pedagogical approach, to make pupils aware of the school's expectations of their behaviour, and to support pupils in managing their own behaviour. Can the learning process be enhanced for all pupils in the classroom with an identified pedagogical approach?

Inclusion

Fundamental to any investigation of pedagogy and learning is the issue of inclusion, and the role it plays within any school. Rather than becoming a tired concept of which much has been written over the past ten years, the search for a common understanding of its meaning in the education community continues apace. For many it has become *de rigueur* for mission statements, political speeches and policy documents of all kinds. It has become a cliché – obligatory in the discourse of all right-thinking people (Cooper 2004). Cooper points out that, when we talk about inclusive education we are also talking about social inclusion, but that in specific terms inclusive education is primarily concerned with the individual's active engagement in formal learning processes.

This establishment of a working definition of inclusion is crucial for the purposes of this book. The book will make continual reference to the engagement by pupils in the learning process and the many barriers, in this case behaviour, which may prevent them from taking a full part in this process. The relationship between learning behaviour and inclusion will illuminate the requirement for all schools to maintain and develop this relationship in the context of the learning process.

Claire Turner (2003) states that her research, conducted within her own school on the effectiveness and inclusiveness of the school's behaviour policy, showed that pupils with emotional behavioural difficulties noted that both their own and the class's learning was affected by their behaviour. She alludes to the fact that she discovered "a discrepancy" between how staff members are supposed to deal with poor behaviour (as laid out in the school's behaviour policy) and what actually happens in lessons. There may be a number of reasons for this, which might beg such questions as:

- How is the behaviour policy administered?
- What level of ownership do staff members feel for the policy?
- Is the policy deliverable in the present context within the school?
- Are pupils fully aware of and consistently reminded of the policy?
- Is the policy adhered to consistently by everyone throughout the school?

On the question of consistency, Scott-Baumann *et al.* (2002: 333), in a chapter relating to working with pupils with difficulties, advise trainee teachers to show respect, stay calm, and endeavour to be consistent, assertive and positive.

This issue of consistency is pertinent within any educational institution and will be visited throughout this book. Indeed, Ainscow (1995) drew upon findings from the UNESCO Teacher Education project, "Special Needs in the Classroom", to identify the necessary conditions for providing effective education for all, namely effective leadership, which means:

- Involving staff, students and community in policy-making
- Collaborative planning

- Emphasising the potential benefits of enquiry and reflection
- Operating a policy for staff development.

The above list of conditions supports the findings by Stansfield (2003) in his review of Bill Rogers' *A Practical Guide to Effective Teaching, Behaviour Management and Colleague Support* (2002). Stansfield quotes Rogers' assertion that "The whole school policy of shared values, aims and practices about managing behaviour is important when supporting individual teachers in their classroom management". He continues by recommending Rogers' book to all teachers, trainees, newly qualified teachers and experienced teachers as "a guide to exploring the fundamentals of good teaching".

Can the learning process be enhanced for all pupils in the classroom with an identified pedagogical approach?

The notion of shared aims, values and practices is vital to ensure the paradigm shift towards an emotionally intelligent school. How then can this be achieved?

The DfE circular (DfE 1994), often referred to as the "six pack", suggests that the whole school approach to behaviour management should incorporate:

- Simplicity, straightforwardness, specificity; based on clear defensible principles and valuing positiveness, set in constructive terms clearly setting out what children can and cannot do.
- Rules, which should be kept to a minimum, and for which the reasons should be clear.

Gribble, quoted in the DfE circular, argued that "such approaches help to maintain the dignity of the teacher and [. . .] by taking these approaches a mutual respect between pupils and teacher can be encouraged".

Haim Ginott, cited in Rogers (2004), maintains that "[t]eachers have the power to affect a child's life for better or worse. A child becomes what he/she experiences [. . .] they [the teachers] can open or close the minds and hearts of children."

This power invested in teachers is very much underestimated by some teachers (or, indeed, at times overestimated by others, who may not always use this power effectively). There is a real difference between exerting power over pupils and exercising power for and pupils.

Rogers (2004) talks about the "self-fulfilling prophecy" of "the Pygmalion effect" whereby pupils can often be categorised as being able to achieve up to a certain level and no further. Too often, expectations are limited by previous knowledge of family, early test results or social deprivation. Is there a common understanding within our profession of the notion of high expectations? Or is it a fact that the low expectations of certain "types" of student by professionals nurture the self-fulfilling prophecy? Within the Teacher Development Authority Qualifying Teacher Standards, there must be at least three standards relating directly to trainee teachers having "high" expectations of their pupils. Is this defined in terms of what exactly is meant by this, and are teachers' expectations fluid or fixed?

In one of the present authors' experience while working for a local authority, having been given the brief of preventing pupil exclusions at Key Stage Three, a staff team meeting was convened for all teachers of Kieran, a pupil in Year 7. The meeting began negatively, with one teacher informing the group that Kieran would not make it to Year 8 because three months previously his brother, a Year 11 pupil, had been permanently excluded. This meant that Kieran would undoubtedly be similar in both ability and outlook, and would suffer the same fate. The intrinsic power of this teacher almost curtailed any remedial work at source. Kieran would disprove the teacher's theory by remaining at the school for the remainder of his school career. He overturned the self-fulfilling prophecy by establishing himself as an individual who would allow external intervention, enabling him to exercise control and influence over his own behaviour in the context of the classroom, with the full support of a group of interested adults.

Cooper (2004) addresses this issue by questioning whether or not the experience of mainstream schooling is in fact the deciding factor as to whether a pupil is "included" or not. He maintains that a pupil with barriers to learning may be emotionally and cognitively excluded by the very nature of a large mainstream school. He concurs that the essential criterion for such a pupil may be to work in a setting where conditions will allow him or her to enjoy maximum social and academic engagement. Much current thought suggests that the issues around expectation and the reaction to children with barriers to their learning can be resolved within the school setting. Therefore a child can have an equally positive experience of mainstream and supported education within its own school. Much work is being done to address the issues of barriers to learning, utilising the strengths and resources of the mainstream school, enabling individual intervention as and when required.

Rogers (2004) refers to colleagues who have worked hard to "devictimise" pupils, not "revictimise" them, and to "Enable these children to believe in themselves and value learning [. . .] to encourage the child to find a positive sense of peer acceptance".

This may be achieved by recognising that the often negative response of some children to work stems from their own barriers to learning, which may be genuine or merely perceived by the child, who may then resort to challenging behaviour as the only way they feel that they can respond. It is their response to being excluded from teaching and learning within the class that affects both their learning progress and that of others in the classroom.

This may be achieved by prioritising the need to develop emotional intelligence both within the classroom and the staffroom. The work of Rogers, particularly in recent years, has centred on the individual's access to learning and breaking down the barriers to learning. In understanding pupils with EBD, he pinpoints as essential not so much the programme provided, but a teacher using whatever teaching strategy and content that makes positive connections in these children's lives. A constant feature of Rogers' published works over the past twenty years has been the recognition of the importance of colleague support. Rogers (1997: 22) believes that making positive use of colleague support in rebuilding good-will and having a sense of shared purpose is essential to the health of every class.

He points to the importance of building long and lasting relationships with the classroom, which for the most part is the responsibility of the education professional but must also be seen as the responsibility of the child.

This is a major issue for schools both in the primary and secondary sector, and is featured throughout Rogers' published work. There appears to be a need for further work on systems for engaging disaffected, demotivated or disinterested colleagues. What Rogers neglects to do in his published works is to suggest practical ways in which staff can be systematically encouraged, cajoled or indeed instructed to incorporate colleague support . This relates directly to the notion of the inclusive school and in particular the role of the leadership in taking all staff with it through effecting significant change by evolving an ethos and culture which embraces an achievable level of inclusion that is accepted and, more importantly, delivered by all staff. This should be regarded as a prerequisite in developing a cohesive, integrated behaviour policy, the benefits of which may transform the health of a school.

Teaching can be an isolating profession on occasions. Throughout his work Rogers refers to the importance of working with colleagues on the teaching and support staff to revisit the health and well-being of each individual class. He advocates a positive stance in an initiative that he describes as a "fresh start". (Rogers 1997). The basic premise of the "fresh start is that any class at any time can be offered a fresh start and a new relationship forged with the class teacher" (Rogers 2004).

The fresh start is introduced through the platform of a class meeting, and the teacher, often supported by TAs or other members of the teaching staff, will conduct an open meeting with the class who are asked up to three key questions such as: "What can/should be done to change things here (so that we can get on with having a classroom where we can learn well without undue noise, calling out, time 'off-task')?"

This question, asked either in the form of a discussion or as a written question to individual children, is then put to the group as a whole. This will be accompanied by some ground rules which might include focusing on the question, making only constructive responses, a one-at-a-time rule and possibly an agreed time limit for individual responses. The importance of such an initiative is that it gives pupils responsibility for their behaviour and allows individuals and the group to comment and consider the status quo (Rogers 2004) They have the power to amend or change the present situation into something which may be more enjoyable, and beneficial for all. Rogers does not comment on frequency of this initiative with one specific class, or indeed whether it is possible to repeat or to incorporate it into the lifestyle of an individual class. He does refer to a follow-up meeting in which feedback and responses to the first meeting may be given. This may be in the form of a class handout. Suggestions might include a change in seating plan, cues for entry into the classroom, cues for engaging TAs, and so on. Rogers also identifies a possible need for individual teachers to reappraise their own leadership, behaviour and discipline in any fresh start.

This pedagogical approach relies on consistency. This consistency is required not just for one class or indeed for one initiative, but rather surrounds a complete behaviour policy and with all classes. This approach is extremely demanding to sustain and requires, within a school, an agreed, sustained approach to all learning situations. Subsequently this will signal to pupils across the school that this may eventually be adopted as the norm as opposed to a one-off initiative.

The secret of success is the ability to survive failure.

(Noël Coward)

It is crucial to point out that children exhibiting challenging behaviour are not set up to fail. Many children can exhibit challenging behaviour this will often be described as secondary behaviour. By secondary behaviour Rogers is referring to behaviour which may be exhibited as a result of the initial misdemeanour not being effectively dealt with by the teacher. This refers to the work of Skinner (cited in Scott-Baumann *et al.* 2002) who underlines the importance of "positive reinforcement" which is manifested by teachers noticing and dealing with positive responses and not allowing pupils the opportunity to repeat antisocial behaviour. It follows that behaviour initiatives lead such pupils towards success and achievement and, just as important, to self-belief. In *Behaviour Recovery* (1994), Rogers, who wrote this book as a whole school programme for mainstream primary pupils, portrays his pragmatic approach to issues of dealing with behavioural issues in primary schools, but addresses directly those pupils displaying behavioural difficulties, in particular their low self-concept and self-esteem. In Chapter 4, "Motivating BD Students", Rogers refers to "BD" children as:

> Children [who]often experience rejection by their peers [. . .] have poor incentive, display minimal effort, are described as socially disruptive [. . .] all the while they are actively seeking their own social place.

These assertions are again underpinned by the work of Skinner (2002) who introduced the theory of Associationism, whereby pupils associate certain behaviours with particular environments in school and are therefore locked into a cycle of mistrust, low self-concept and low self-esteem as a result of being labelled failures by certain teachers, or within the whole school. Rogers continues by alluding to the importance of behaviour recovery as "Strengthening the pupil's belief in his ability to relate socially in positive ways".

The pupil gains strength in being valued, and this behaviour success can increase his value of himself, thus increasing his self-esteem. Rogers continues by stating that the most important motivator is the teacher and the belief that teacher holds in the pupil. This then translates to teacher expectations, discussed above. Rogers maintains that with regard to teacher expectations pupils detect them by:

- The kind of attention given
- Accepting that pupils with behavioural difficulties make mistakes
- The way in which tasks are set
- Getting contributions from pupils in class.

This is an interesting set of criteria but is not necessarily the accepted notion of teacher expectations, which normally convey themselves in assessment of learning or in outcomes such as work produced or contributions made. It was Maslow (1970) who stated that "All children want to belong. It is a primary social need."

This may be true to the extent that children will want to belong to something which is rewarding, perceived to be somewhere they can succeed and not feel that the price to pay for belonging is to be punished and rewarded at regular intervals. Unfortunately, some children believe that they can only belong when they are drawing attention to themselves, or engaging teachers in power struggles.

Rogers (2004) claims that all teachers hold great power within their gift with all classes, even those which are most demanding and time consuming (Ginott 1971). It is how this power is used which dictates the classroom environment and the conditions whereby successful teaching and learning consistently takes place. Power and effectiveness as a teacher are inextricably linked. To pause for analogy, and to demonstrate this concept in an equally influential arena, I had the pleasure recently of witnessing a football referee admonishing a young player for a misdemeanour in what was a keenly contested game. Following this appropriate intervention, the referee inexplicably continued to berate this player and belittle him in front of what was a sizeable group of spectators of all ages. To the young man's credit he decided not to respond or indeed communicate with the referee in any way: a good example of misuse and abuse of power by an official supported by a clear code of conduct designed to protect both official and player. The analogy is self-explanatory and serves to highlight the potential of abusing power, and also the possibility of long-term damage caused by the teacher/referee with a heavy responsibility and duty of care. As Rogers (2004) explains:

> "the teacher has the power to motivate [. . .] assist, engage, teach and encourage".

Kyriacou (1991) ventures further on the issue of teacher power and influence, stating that "The ability to teach and lead effectively is about wanting and learning to be an effective teacher". The common thread here is the danger for teachers of underestimating their influence at whatever stage of their teaching career. Individuals can have the same dramatic effect upon pupils whether in positions of senior responsibility or teaching a class once a fortnight in a PSHE lesson. The notion of time is extremely complex in all phases of education. At secondary level it has been said that it is increasingly difficult for teachers to give pupils any time beyond the classroom commitment. It is more a case of how important teachers view additional contact in the form of team sports, arts-based clubs, or merely acknowledging pupils around the school. It remains an interesting exercise to ask those within the profession: Just what is teaching all about?

In his book *Teacher Leadership and Behaviour Management* (2002) Rogers refers to "Take-up time" and its importance in allowing pupils time and space within the classroom. They are able to digest teacher input, accept or reject suggestions and to implement intervention without escalation of a situation or loss of face.

Take up time operates at the kernel of successful educational exchange between teacher and pupil. Many teachers operate with anger, and indeed there are times when guarded anger can be most effective. Rogers (2002) states in relation to teacher anger: "If we overdo anger we devalue the moral currency and weight of anger."

Skinner (2002) maintains that teachers "Ensure the repetition of unacceptable behaviour by expending a good deal of time, energy and attention in punishment." This "relationship" between teacher and pupils is referred to by Robertson (1996) (cited in Rogers 2002) and supports the notion introduced in the Elton Report (1989) of the importance of "reasoning with a pupil or pupils outside the classroom setting".

Brighouse (2006) refers to the importance of "teachers outside the classroom". This reference alludes to the importance of teachers regarding themselves as being influential in the lives of pupils in the corridor, in the playground and at lunchtime.

Robertson sees the priority as being an attempt to fix the problem as opposed to issuing detention or some other sanction. This would again hinge rather acutely on the state of the relationship between pupils(s) and teacher. Kounin (1970) (cited by Rogers 2002) reflects on the concept of teacher authority and its importance within the classroom, particularly how it is viewed by both teacher and pupils: "Authority is essentially an agreement between teachers and students and without this, teachers do not have sufficient power to wrest control from the ringleaders to enforce order."

It is an interesting concept that authority, before being accepted by both parties, has to be allowed and negotiated rather than imposed merely because of the teacher's status. This may be construed by some as an example of weakness and over-compromise. It would appear however to be essential if one accepts the importance of the development of a positive working relationship between pupil(s) and teacher. Kounin (1970) (cited in Rogers 2002) reflects on the reasons for disruption in class in the light of his comments on authority, and maintains that disruption occurs mainly "[w]hen students were waiting, either physically, not having the knowledge or resources to get on with the task, or intellectually [. . .] because they were bored".

It is within these gaps that minor or even major disruption can occur, highlighting quite clearly the importance of planning, using resources including effective assistance of other adults in the classroom, and also carefully planned differentiation. This use of teaching assistants touched upon by Rogers in his major works albeit in the current climate with insufficient depth, though he makes consistent references to the education community and its role in the positive development of the pupil's education career. One of the gold standards of Rogers' approach to classroom behaviour and a prerequisite in his opinion for consistently successful pedagogical intervention is that of colleague support.

The Elton Report (Elton 1989) referred to the problem of "teacher isolation". Fullan and Hargreaves (1991) (cited in Rogers 2002), within the realm of their extensive work on school improvement, cite the importance of questioning whether collegiality is always good. Fullan expresses the view that "seeking to eliminate individualism, we should not eliminate individuality.[. . .] We cannot mandate, what matters is effective practice [. . .] the more complex the change, the less you can force it" (Fullan 1993).

It remains the case that each individual school fosters its own culture, though teacher leadership and collaboration dictate the development of that culture, particularly with regard to the extent to which the staff feel ownership of the culture. It was George Eliot, cited in Rogers (2002), who posed the question: "What do we live for if it is not to make life less difficult for each other?"

Rogers (2002) supports this by reflecting that:

> When a school leadership consciously values, affirms, models and develops supportive options, structures [. . .] then there is a basis for an ecology of support [. . .] then our teaching will have that professional collegiality necessary for professional assurance and professional esteem.

This assertion forms the backdrop to much of the work of Rogers, who places great store by the conditions necessary for excellent teaching and learning to take place. The issue of professional assurance and self-esteem is complex, and requires a school culture which is both confident and all-embracing for staff. School leaders are required to continually question its ethos and relevance to the school, and to the wider community.

Rogers (1997), in relation to the importance of collegiality in addressing the specific issue of working with challenging pupils, believes that, as staff, "We are more effective when we have addressed the hard class issue whole school [. . .] we need the support of our peers to crack the hard class."

Conclusion

In the training of teachers, in which I have previously been involved, great emphasis is placed upon the fact that as teachers we are never alone and have the support of mentors, department colleagues, heads of year, heads of department, senior staff and the headteacher. This can only be translated with confidence by a trainee teacher if he or she personally experiences this "collegiality and support". It is no less important for experienced colleagues to acknowledge this support and revisit their own particular role in the culture within which they operate, both individually and collectively.

New teachers entering the profession may find themselves daunted by the enormity of the task awaiting them in developing and adopting particular strategies and pedagogical approaches, particularly in the light of the number of behaviour programmes being introduced in secondary schools in particular, including the Behaviour for Learning programme with specific guidelines on procedure, rewards and punishment. This works to a certain extent in complete contrast to the Behaviour 4 Learning programme commissioned by the Teacher Development Agency which emphasises the pedagogical role in creating a positive learning environment. For the emotionally literate school to thrive and prosper, the following should be in place and embraced by the whole school community:

- Building relationships with pupils
- Understanding all pupils who experience barriers to their learning
- Defining and retaining genuine high expectations for all pupils
- Strong school leadership/teacher leadership
- Promoting and receiving consistent colleague support
- Building a supportive ecology in schools.

It also begins to address the question: Can the learning process be enhanced for all pupils in the classroom with an identified pedagogical approach?

As to whether the learning process is enhanced by the above, only extensive school-based research will reveal answers to this question.

Teaching styles

> Education is not filling a pail but the lighting of a fire.
>
> William Butler Yeats[5]

> Education: (Latin) *educare* "bring up", related to *educere* "bring out potential" and *ducere* "to lead".

Every teacher is unique, just as every child is unique. We have looked at Gardner's Multiple Intelligences in the context of how children learn and how teachers teach from their preferred learning styles, but what of your personal physical demeanour and attitude to teaching? When we analyse what "education" means we see that its Latin root *educere* and *ducere* mean to "lead the bringing out of potential". The word education did not originally mean the act or process of imparting knowledge. It does not mean to feed in but to lead out. This original etymological understanding of the word puts a different perspective on the role of the educator. The educator leads the bringing out of the child's potential, encouraging the child to come forward with their knowledge of the world and themselves to meet the learning. It is not "I know this and I need you to/would like you to learn this" but "What about this? Can you see what this is? Can we understand how it works? What sense can you make of it?"

If we work from the premise that every child has potential that we are *leading out* with the learning experience, we are respecting and empowering them. We are enquiring into the learning *with* them and not teaching from a pedestal of knowledge. You must remember how powerful you are to your pupils, who already see you as a font of knowledge. A teacher who wraps the mystique of knowledge around themselves to keep a safe teacher–pupil distance may have difficulty in connecting the children to the learning, or may only connect the most secure and able children to the learning.

How do you feel about teaching? Do you still feel as you did when you first came into it with your skills and hopes? When I asked this question to one of the teachers I interviewed she had to admit that she hadn't really reflected on this in her twenty years of teaching: "You don't really get the time to think about yourself, you are always thinking about the children" (Hawkins 2010). She later thanked me for the conversations we had because they gave her a chance to reflect upon her practice and her progression. It is essential that teachers get a chance to talk about their professional progression, how they feel about their teaching and the stresses that are placed upon them. The children become the focus of the school world, of meetings, planning and strategies, and because of time pressures and the desire of teachers to support the children they do not see their own needs met. Support is essential, but so is sharing and talking about practice and praxis: how you teach and the techniques you use and the support you need to develop your sense of enjoyment in the classroom. If the teacher is unfulfilled, stressed or not invigorated by teaching, the children and the school will suffer, and so will the teacher. Let us look at teachers' teaching styles and reflect upon ourselves.

How you position yourself in the classroom environment is crucial. You will have your preferred learning style from which to work. In a workshop I was running with teachers one asked me, during an exercise, to turn down some music that was playing. Another teacher in the group asked, "What music?" For one teacher the music was invasive to her concentration, to the other it was inaudible. One of those teachers would be using music in the classroom because she liked it; the other commented that she wouldn't think about doing a visualisation to music or playing a piece during a break because it wasn't something she was interested in.

One teacher whom I observed in the classroom was quite nervous, and because of her tension clenched her hands into fists. When she made gestures they were sharp and with a tense, flat hand. I mimed back her teaching stance and asked her how my personality came across. "Aggressive," she replied, obviously rather shocked. We talked about how her nerves were affecting her teaching persona and set about ways in which she could release her tension. She ended up using a bean bag that she kept on her desk for circle time. She would hold this at the start of a lesson when talking to the children. As her confidence grew and she relaxed, the bean bag was returned to the desk.

In another instance a teacher who was chiefly linguistic-logical said she worked with a whiteboard for 80 per cent of her delivery but was not so confident about working with a more kinaesthetic interaction with the children. She felt she was in a strong position when teaching from the board and would be unable to handle the "chaos" of the children moving about. Being still and having the children focus on the board made her feel she was in control. She felt she could get the information over to her pupils and that they could see the facts. She used pictures and photographs and back-up sheets. She believed her teaching was limited to the board and wanted to open it up. She worked in well-held short bursts at the ends of lessons with experiential techniques and built up her confidence. I admired her ability to assess her teaching and her courage to try new techniques.

We have to think about what tools we might not be utilising in our teaching and allow ourselves the possibility that they might be useful to us and fun to

TABLE 2.1 Teaching style – positions

Teaching position	What the position says	Teacher–pupil relationship	Child's perception of teaching position
Teacher behind desk.	I am the teacher. I will come to you when I am ready.	Table becomes a barrier between you and the children. Sense of control and safety for the teacher.	The teacher has other things to do. The teacher is separated from me. I have to approach the teacher.
Teacher is sitting on, or by the side of the desk.	I am the teacher, I am open to you.	Greater sense of availability. Less formal position.	The teacher is open to me.
Whiteboard delivery. Teacher standing at the whiteboard.	I am the teacher. The learning takes place on the whiteboard and also with me. I give you the learning.	The whiteboard supports me. The whiteboard is interesting. The whiteboard keeps me separate from the children. I can give a lot of information to the children.	I have to look and read. Learning is fast and can change quickly. The board teaches me things. The board is important. The board goes wrong sometimes. We are a class.
Teacher standing at board – pupils on floor.	I am the teacher. I am powerful.	I can see them all – they are listening and in one group. Distanced from children.	My neck hurts, I am not comfortable. The teacher is tall. I receive the learning.
Desk configuration changes for different lessons.	The teacher changes the environment. The teacher wants to make things interesting.	These lessons are different and we need to approach them in different ways. The classroom adapts to the learning.	The teacher likes to change things for different lessons. Things look different. Something different will happen. We learn in different ways.
Children sit in a circle on the floor. Teacher on chair sitting in the circle. Backs to desks when necessary.	I am the teacher working with you at your level. We are in this together.	Team working. Moments at the same level of learning.	The teacher is with us and available to us. I can see them clearly. They are working with me on my level.
Teacher moves among children when working, gaining eye contact and smiling.	I am the teacher. I am supporting you one to one.	We work together. I am looking out for each of you.	The teacher is available. The teacher is helping ME. I am important and OK.

use. When a teacher is stretched and stressed by the requirements placed upon them it may seem impossible to try new techniques other than what you believe works in the classroom. Why move out of your comfort zone? Some reasons might be to energise yourself, to open up new possibilities, to engage your pupils in different ways, to refresh your teaching and to give yourself a chance to develop and learn new techniques. Teachers are constantly asked to deliver to their pupils but are rarely delivered to. When was the last time you thought about yourself as a developing professional practitioner? Read through the following questions and reflect on your answers; there is no multiple choice or correct answer, just a chance for you to assess how you operate in your professional practice.

Thinking about your teaching style

DO YOU TALK A LOT? If you do, are you stopping to check that the children understand what you are saying? They will remember only 20 per cent of what they hear without other input.

DO YOU TALK TOO FAST? Children have different processing speeds. If you are talking or reading a story, try and listen to yourself and use your voice as a tool to get the story or points across. If you use the technique of *wanting* to get every ounce of the story across to the children and trying to paint the pictures of the story with your voice, you will slow down.

DO YOU HAVE A VOICE PEOPLE LIKE TO LISTEN TO? WELL MODULATED, CONFIDENT? We have a three-and-a-half-octave speaking range. When nervous, many women speak in the higher point of their range. It is important to use the range of your voice and the level and tone. It is a great tool for you regarding your teaching delivery. Your feelings are expressed through your vocal quality. A voice can encourage, calm and warn. It is a major part of the way in which you signal to children. They will read the tonal quality of your voice as much as what you say to them. I have worked with very soft-spoken teachers who create a sense of calm and expectation where the children respond to the quietness and mirror it. I have also worked with very vocally confident teachers who sing-song requests and change the tempo and colour of their voice to engage their pupils. You will have your vocal comfort zone but experiment with your level and inflections. If you do get nervous, breathe and relax, and try placing your voice lower to stop your pitch rising. If you often speak in a tired voice this may well be through stress and tension, causing you to catch your voice in the throat. It may help to hum in the mornings and gently warm up your vocal cords before you start teaching. I remember one teacher who would have a "whisper morning" when all the children had to talk very quietly and listen hard.

DO YOU DELIVER YOUR TEACHING WITH A SMILE OR MORE FORMALLY? Smiles are powerful as a social sign of safety and acceptance. Children will often respond by smiling back. Children will attune to your mood and want to feel secure with you; if you are relaxed and happy they will relax. Don't worry that if you smile too much you lose control because you become too accessible, you just become safer.

WHERE DO YOU LIKE TO POSITION YOURSELF IN THE CLASSROOM? Think of where you like to place yourself in the classroom. Have you a designated area that is your own space? Do you change where you sit? Do you move around a lot in the classroom or do you prefer to be anchored in one place? Do you sit behind or at the side of a desk? The teaching positions shown in Table 2.1 demonstrate the meanings of various positions and stances in the classroom. Reflect on how you teach and what it would be like to be a child in your classroom.

HOW MANY DIFFERENT WAYS DO YOU GET POINTS/FACTS ACROSS TO THE CHILDREN? Do you lean towards one way of teaching or do you combine different techniques? Do you use music, kinaesthetic techniques, food, art, science and so on across all subjects? Do you rely on one or two main ways to deliver your teaching, or many various ways? Do all of the children in your class engage with your teaching?

DO YOU WATCH YOURSELF TEACHING? Do you assess your teaching after a lesson? How did it go? Did I try something new? Was that as successful as I hoped?

DO YOU SET CLEAR AND SAFE BOUNDARIES? Are you clear about what you expect from the children? Do you negotiate these rules and boundaries with them? What strategies do you have in place to support your rules for acceptable behaviour? Have the children got ownership of these rules?

DO YOU LAUGH WITH THE CHILDREN? Laughter only happens when everyone is safe and attuned. It is a great tool for connecting with the children and socialising the class. If you find humour difficult have a joke book and a joke minute after tidying up the classroom, during a break or at the end of a lesson before playtime. Understanding humour often takes good processing skills and wit.

HOW OFTEN DO YOU CHANGE YOUR CLASSROOM TO CREATE A NEW SPACE FOR WORK? Changing the classroom space is invigorating for all. Use the initial process as a problem-solving test and get the children to work out how they can move the furniture to give you a central space for experiential work. Changing the space energises the children and allows you to adjust your teaching position and relationship with the children.

DO YOU APPROBATE GOOD BEHAVIOUR/WORK FROM ALL CHILDREN – OR MOSTLY THE CHALLENGING ONES? This is an easy trap to fall into. The lesson with a challenging child behaving well is such a relief that we want to approbate and encourage the behaviour. A teacher at a special school told me a story about a school trip that staff members were dreading, since one boy was extremely challenging whenever he was in a public place. He did very well, and on their return the staff said how pleased they had been with his behaviour and that they had praised him. "Did you praise the others?" one teacher asked. All the children had found the trip challenging but everyone had done well. We often forget the good work or behaviours that come from the consistently well-behaved children in our classes because the challenging children, by necessity, get so much of our attention (Miles 2009).

HOW MUCH DO YOU LET THE CHILDREN TALK? This is an interesting question, as I have often worked with teachers who believe that children have an input into the lesson but who cut their answers short. You will have a budding Cicero[6] in your class who needs to be curtailed but I have seen children refused the offer to finish a teacher's question in order to save time. This is very destructive to some children who will feel they are slow and who will stop making those offers. Listening to and approbating children is a huge boost for their self-esteem; your interaction with them is a very important part of their social standing in the school and their skills for life.

DO YOU LET THE CHILDREN REFLECT ON THE LEARNING OR DO IT FOR THEM? Reflection, especially for experiential work, is when the true learning takes place. Children have experienced something, and possibly had an emotional response to it. They then reason the response when they reflect and achieve an understanding of that emotional experience. This is when the thinking and assessing is happening and when the deeper learning is taking place.

DO YOU FEEL AS IF YOU ARE WORKING TO THE CLOCK OR AT YOUR OWN PACE? Don't be led by the clock. It is stressful and you will feel defeated if you "never finish anything". Pace your lessons to the children and take the time you and the children need. You must judge the best pace of work for the best learning outcomes for your children; you are in control in the classroom.

HAVE YOU ASKED THE CHILDREN WHAT AND HOW THEY WOULD TEACH FOR A DAY? This is a great way to see the classroom through the children's eyes. With older children you could group them into teams and get each team to teach the class for a lesson. This gives you an insight into how they perceive education and what and how they would like to be taught. It gives the children an insight into what it is like to teach. You and your TA could be the challenging ones at the back of the class for a change!

ARE YOU WORKING TO THE PACE OF THE MORE ABLE CHILDREN OR TO THE PACE OF THE LESS ABLE? DO YOU RESENT THE LESS ABLE CHILDREN WHO SLOW YOU DOWN? IF YOU DO, HOW DO YOU COPE WITH THAT FRUSTRATION? This is the Catch-22 situation because as the range of ability and need stretches wider the teacher has to decide where to pitch the teaching. Even with the help of the TA, managing the needs of all children is very difficult. The reaction to this question depends upon how the teacher perceives their role and what being successful in it means. A teacher who wants to achieve may feel that the less able children are preventing them from realising their teaching potential. They might feel they are being stretched too widely, or are being asked to be a SEN teacher when they are not a specialist. If you do resent the less able children then you need to talk with a mentor because the frustration that stems from this situation will affect your teaching and your well-being. The teacher, as well as the children, needs support in this situation.

DO YOU SEE YOURSELF PROGRESSING IN YOUR PRACTICE? Taking the time to reflect is important for your development as a teacher. How do you teach and what would you like to develop? Where do you feel you restrict yourself and where can you identify areas that you want to strengthen? Taking time to reflect on your practice is important for you as an educator and as a person working in a highly important, pressurised field.

Thinking about your support

If a child's behaviour issues are wearing you out you need to be able to develop new strategies for dealing with the behaviour or talk through your worries with someone who can support and understand you. We are quick to set up nurture groups for children in our environment but we do not do the same for the adults who are on the front line, working with and trying to connect with these children, which can be extremely draining for the adults who interact with them. I have worked with teachers who have said that they feel it would be a sign of weakness to "admit" that they cannot cope with a difficult child in their class.

Some issues may be out of our control but a great deal is within our control when we allow ourselves the time to think about what we need to function well in our work, to allow *ourselves* to realise our full potential. Think about what support you have in place:

- Do you get support when you feel stressed and under pressure?
- Do you share your plans and ideas with other teachers?
- Do you share your worries with other teachers? Talk about school and class issues?
- Is your headteacher supportive? Do they listen and put positive help into place?
- Do you feel isolated or part of a team?
- Do you ever get time to review your practice?
- How do you give yourself time to stop and relax during the teaching day or year?
- Do you constantly work late preparing for the next day while at home?
- How do you look after yourself? Do you relax and recharge away from school?

If support networks are not in place for you then it is worth looking at what can be provided and how other schools support their teachers. You may be a well-knit group of teachers and TAs who socialise and talk easily. You may have a separation between TAs and teachers, between the Infant and the Junior sections of the school. This does not help an integrated delivery of learning for the children. The teaching staff need to be able to share information and worries about pupils and celebrate and share what works in their practice.

Be aware that it is easy to get into work patterns that can exhaust you: pushing yourself through the day and not having a break as you prepare the next lesson, and feeling you are totally reactive to the needs of children and management. A balance between work and the quality of your life outside work is essential for your emotional well-being and the quality of your delivery. In the emotionally intelligent classroom teachers must take care of their own needs as well as the children's.

3 Teaching Vulnerable Children

> An understanding heart is everything in a teacher and cannot be esteemed highly enough. One looks back with appreciation to the brilliant teachers, but with gratitude to those who touched our human feelings. The curriculum is so much necessary raw material, but warmth is the vital element for the growing plant and for the soul of the child.
>
> Carl Jung[1]

Trauma: Greek τραῦμα (*trauma*), meaning damage or wound.

A separate chapter on vulnerable children in a book that deals with emotional and social intelligence is a little like delivering your SEAL directives in a one-session block: unrealistic. You are always teaching the social and emotional aspects of learning through your delivery, whatever the lesson. In addition, one might suggest that all children are vulnerable to differing degrees regarding their level of powerlessness in most of their dealings with adults. We must acknowledge the control and power we have in a teacher–child relationship at primary level, but we must also acknowledge that we will be working with children who have a past or present history that may severely limit their ability to learn.

Let us define "vulnerable children", which isn't easy, since the term is used in different contexts. It is not defined in the Children Act 1989, where the terms "child in need" and "child at risk of significant harm" are used. The term "vulnerable child" has been utilised to cover both of these definitions (a child at risk of significant harm is automatically a child in need of services). The Welsh Assembly[2] has included a definition of the term "vulnerable children" as meaning children:

■ who are unlikely to achieve or maintain, or have the opportunity of achieving or maintaining, a reasonable standard of health or development without the provision for them of social care services

- whose health or development is likely to be significantly impaired, or further impaired, without the provision for them of social care services
- who have a physical or mental impairment
- who are in the care of a public authority
- who are provided with accommodation by a public authority in order to secure their well-being.

(House of Commons Welsh Affairs Committee 2009)

In terms of behaviour, a child who has been taken into the care system and is looked after by the local authority or who has been adopted and has moved out of the care system, the emotional damage that has been inflicted on them by their prime caregivers will continue to give them issues regarding their sense of safety, their sense of self and their ability to function in a social world. This will have a huge affect upon their behaviour in the classroom.

We have talked a great deal about the necessity of creating safety in the school environment and how important this is for the transition of a child from home to the school environment. Children who have learnt to regulate their stress and impulses through their secure attachment to their parents will be able to use these skills to cope with their new environment. When this is achieved the child will feel safe to function, to connect and to gain a sense of belonging to school and be motivated and open to the learning experience. Those children who are not securely attached to their parents, who have lost their parents through being taken into care, who have been physically, emotionally or sexually abused or neglected by their parents will very likely be unable to regulate their stress and impulses and will have great difficulty with the mammoth exercise of coping with a new environment, adults, other children and learning. Bereaved children have also suffered loss and separation from the parent and will be traumatised by this event.

As adults we see life from our own point of view, from the expectations that were formed for us through our experiences when we were children. Some of us may be able to understand the deep vulnerability of a traumatised child. Some of us may be able to empathise and pitch our behaviour and treatment of the child at an appropriate level. Some of us may find it difficult to acknowledge what might have happened to the child and treat that child in the same way as we treat other children in our class and wonder at the behaviour that comes back to us.

One of the problems cited by adopters has been the lack of teachers' capability to listen to their child's history. This is called "avoidance" and may arise because a teacher feels uncomfortable about talking about the specific abuse that the child suffered, or feels it is inappropriate to discuss the child's history or that it is in the past and the child must "move on". Very often adopters are told that their child will be "all right now it has a family and people to love them". This may be because we want the child to be "all right" and to find a happy ending of love and safety, but for children who have suffered at the hands of their prime carers this path can take a lifetime – your interventions, care and understanding are crucial to this damaged human being.

This is mirrored by government policy in the way that looked-after children are at the top of the list for schools submission, but the adopted child (who will carry the same issues regarding trauma and post-traumatic stress disorder and fear of new environments) is not on that list. There is no "make-it-all-right machine" for children who have suffered varying forms of abuse and neglect; there is only time and care, and the slow building of their resilience towards owning their own life and the chance of finding safety and some level of enjoyment in it. The degree of success which these children will have is totally dependent upon the adults and services to which they have access. The schools and their teachers are crucial in this process.

Trauma

When children experience trauma through witnessing or suffering abusive events it affects their lives and well-being. It has a deeply wounding and lasting impact upon their minds, their personalities and their bodies. When a child suffers from post-traumatic stress disorder it impairs their memory, their ability to empathise and to socialise, their resilience, their processing, their sense of self, and their ability to trust and to learn. They may resemble any other child in the playground apart from perhaps being more active or more withdrawn, but they are not functioning like other children. They may be in a state of constant hyper-arousal or "watchfulness", expecting danger at every moment, and their bodies will react in a strong physiological way to imagined dangers. Such children will have had their expectations of adult behaviour formed by dangerous adults; they will not readily trust or feel safe in any environment, or believe that, initially, you will not be a danger to them. We may follow Maslow's Hierarchy of Needs and create a calm and safe environment but the traumatised child will not necessarily believe that it is safe or will remain safe. Only consistency and time will begin to build the belief in the child that safety can exist. If their home life was chaotic they will feel uncomfortable with order and calm, they will want to create what they know and expect and may attempt to illicit aggressive reactions from you through their aggressive behaviour. Chaos is more comfortable than calm to a child who has only known chaos and they will try and create it where they can. When you are faced with these behaviours in your classroom you will need to identify them and separate them from your feelings about the child. There are reasons for these behaviours; the child who is seemingly flouting your authority and "winding you up" or not doing what you ask is confused and in a state of confusion. You must see the behaviours as a consequence of extremely damaging experience and work to see through them to the injured child. You must use your emotional intelligence, your reasoning and clear thinking to work out strategies and ways to engage with the child and then to engage them in learning. It may be that the greatest thing you can teach them is trust in a caring adult.

Triggers and avoidance

This "triggering" of the fear reaction is something that traumatised children live with every moment of their lives. They will avoid anything that may trigger the re-experiencing of traumatic stress:

> They avoid lunches, or certain foods, or eating. They may avoid having baths, or going to the toilet, or going to bed, or getting up or people in green cars. In short, anything at all that might ever have acted as a prompt to a highly sensitive limbic system may come to be the next object of avoidance.
>
> (Cairns 2002)

The problem with the triggered response is that it leaps from one object to another. For example, if an abusive experience was preceded by a tap on the door, a child painting in an art lesson may hear a tap on the door and the trigger then becomes the smell of paint, or the prospect of an art lesson and so on (Cairns 2002). You may not know what action or sound it was that made a vulnerable child in your class suddenly change from being engaged with your lesson to hiding under the table and chewing its shoe, standing like a statue in a corner seemingly unseeing and unhearing, or suddenly screaming and kicking out.

You will recognise this swift emotional physical reaction in some children in your classroom who "jump" at an unexpected sound. Children who have experienced trauma or who live in dangerous environments develop "hyper-vigilance". They are constantly on the look-out for danger, and are often described as being "watchful". Let us look in more detail at how a vulnerable child from an unsafe, traumatic background is functioning.

Hyper-arousal and the fight-or-flight response[3]

Hyper-arousal is unregulated stress which affects the entire body physiologically. In older children hyper-arousal will usually lead to a fight-or-flight response; in younger children hyper-arousal will lead to a freeze response: "an extreme attachment behaviour, demonstrating to any available adult the urgent need to attend to a child too threatened to cry out" (Cairns 2002).

The brain is wired to assess any circumstance for danger. When the threat of danger is seen the brain works very fast to transmit that danger through the eyes to the thalamus[4] which sends it on to the cerebral cortex: its first port of call is the amygdala[5] which is our "danger" filter. Thus this information about danger has two routes: one to the amygdala and one to the conscious brain that will reason out the level of danger. Once a danger is perceived the amygdala prepares the body to work at an optimum level to avoid the danger; in other words a fast physical reaction priming the body for action. The action will be fight, flight or appeasement, i.e. you will face the danger, run away from the danger or try to placate or calm down the danger. A child facing a dangerous situation will look to the parent for safety; if the danger is coming from the parent the child has nowhere to go and will often freeze, producing a state of catatonia. The path to the amygdala and the fight-or-flight response is shorter than the path to the conscious reasoning and consequently our emotional reactions are faster than our conscious ones (Carter, 1999).

Our first reaction to any situation is an emotional one.

When we enter a new room we make emotional judgements about our level of safety or comfort in that room. When we meet a new person we make instant emotional judgements as to whether they are safe and our level of comfort with them, sometimes taking an "instant" like or dislike to them. The way they look is being assessed by our emotional receivers which in turn allow us to feel comfortable or not. If that person were to suddenly produce a sharp knife we would have an immediate emotional fear reaction to it (our eyes send the image of the person and the knife to our amygdala which instantly registers danger). The person steps towards us (our amygdala has already triggered a fast physical reaction and we are ready to get out of the way). The person then places the knife on a table next to a cheese board that we have not seen. The amygdala sends a clear image to the conscious brain for a reasoned response. We would then understand the context of the knife and literally reason our fear away.

When working with looked-after and adopted children you may be dealing with a child who has undergone a traumatic experience or many traumatic experiences. They may be any of the following: physical, psychological, sexual abuse, death of a parent/both parents or witnessing domestic violence, or possibly a mixture of all these experiences. The child may well have suffered and survived experiences that we would find appalling.

In a traumatic event the amygdala initiates the fight-or-flight response and the body goes into action to operate at an optimum level to help us survive the danger. Adrenalin speeds up our heart and raises our blood pressure, and the body produces cortisol which switches off the emergency responses. This bodily reaction will subside and regulate over a few hours, but for the child who has suffered many traumatic experiences through violence and abuse and then the expectation of violence and abuse, the amygdala becomes over-sensitised. This state of hyper-arousal or hyper-vigilance can be triggered again and again.

> Cortisol that floods the brain during prolonged stress is toxic to the brain and can be responsible for hippocampal damage, interfering with feedback systems and the adaptability of the brain.
>
> (Gerhardt 2004)

Teachers often call children with hyper-vigilance "watchful": they seem to be looking out for something. They are primed for danger; it has been set up in their "expectations" of life and behaviour. They will not be able to interact with you or other children in a normal way; they are constantly on the look-out for what may harm them. The amygdala is constantly hijacking the brain and strengthening the fear pathways when anything vaguely reminiscent of the original trauma occurs (Golman 1996).

Fight-or-flight response: visible effects

The body's fight-or-flight reaction will include the following:

- Paling or flushing
- Inhibition of the lacrimal gland (hard to cry – dry mouth)
- Breathing accelerates (fast breathing, hyper-ventilation)
- Bladder relaxes (child may wet)
- Colon relaxes (child may soil)
- Shaking
- Acceleration of instant reflex (child may hit out)
- Auditory exclusion (child may not hear what you are saying)
- Tunnel vision (child may not acknowledge you).

Fight-or-flight response: physiological effects

The body's fight-or-flight reactions will include the following:

- Cortisol released (depresses the immune system)
- Constriction of blood-vessels in many parts of the body
- Adrenalin released (heightened awareness of surroundings)
- Digestion slows down
- Liver releases glucose to provide energy for muscles
- Lack of oxygen to the brain which in the long term will affect short-term memory.

Behaviour in the classroom

You will find that the child is likely to:

- Not act age appropriately (due to lack of developmental input)
- Need to be near you if they perceive you as a safe person
- Have difficulty focusing on anything for any length of time
- Jump at loud noises, be frightened of any shouting and "switch off"
- Be unpredictable in behaviour
- Either be very rejecting of you or want to cuddle you a lot
- Have difficulty remembering instructions
- Be extremely ashamed if singled out under any circumstances (even positive ones)
- Not want to answer the register or offer comments

- Be very watchful and have difficulty sitting still (agitated)
- Be easily distracted by sounds and movements
- Have difficulty processing information (this may affect language and numbers).

The teacher needs to:

- Create a calm space for the child
- Treat the child like a flight animal, namely to be physically and vocally calm (a horse will flee at any sense of danger)
- Acknowledge the child constantly with smiles and reassurance
- Always let the child know the structure of the day – there are no surprises
- Place the child near them at circle times
- Place the child at a table with their back close to a wall to lessen the fear of what may be behind them (it's one less thing for them to worry about)
- Always introduce new adults to the class (strangers can trigger fear responses)
- Give out information about any tasks slowly and clearly, and with visual aids
- Help to build the child's resilience through small projects (such as delivering the register to the office or taking a message) but always scaffold the child with an able partner
- Praise constantly and quietly
- Give the child ways to let you know whether they are worried and that do not attract attention to the child (see Chapter 8)
- Work with a TA to support the child (continuity of the same TA through the school years can aid the child's sense of safety)
- Help the child to use language for feelings and emotions, letting them make up their own (e.g. wobbly, funny tummy, fire tummy), and build up the vocabulary, but always use their words on a Feeling Square (see Chapter 8)
- Make sure the child is safe at playtime (the playground is a potentially dangerous, unstructured, noisy environment).

Dissociation – the "invisible" child

The other reaction to trauma is dissociation. Dissociation can be a response to trauma that allows the mind to distance itself from experiences that are too much for the psyche to process at that time: "Symptoms of dissociation resulting from trauma may include depersonalization, psychological numbing, disengagement, or amnesia regarding the events of the abuse" (Myers 2002). The child is splitting from its traumatic experience in order to survive. These children will be very cut off from any social interaction, having a low sense of self. They dissociate or "cut off" from their own feelings, thoughts and memories.

When working with children who dissociate one often wonders "who is in there?" They may hover around the edges of a classroom and rarely if ever make a vocal offer; they may find it difficult to interact socially and make friends. They will find it difficult to ask you for help, either socially or with their learning.

The dissociated child in your class will often be "invisible" in the classroom; they do not want to be noticed. They do not present with behavioural problems as the child with hyper-arousal – fight or flight – will. The dissociated child will be quiet and get on with their work to the best of their ability. They will not want to be focused on.

> "Our daughter was very withdrawn, she had suffered from severe neglect and a violent environment and it all happened before she could speak.[6] We adopted her when she was three. She had global delay[7] and was at a special school but moved into mainstream education where she is average in a lot of her lessons, which is fantastic considering her start, but we believe she has a lot more potential. She's not getting the help to catch up, she enjoys learning. At one parents' evening a teacher said to us that she was lovely to have in the class and no trouble: "you wouldn't know she was there". She has a kind of invisibility when she's in a group of people. She isn't socially good with other children because she doesn't really know how to fit in. She's not on a level with them socially; she's still having her young childhood because she missed so much of it. We've got private support for her now because she won't get it in school and she deserves to be up there with the other children because she's bright."
>
> Adopters (2010)

There is an issue in education for children who dissociate and who need emotional and educational support. The hyper-aroused fight-or-flight child will "act out" their inner turmoil; it is evident in their behaviour and you will have to put strategies in place to help contain that behaviour and support the child – their anguish is evident. The dissociated child will "act in". They are trying to split away from their trauma, and as they do so they cut off their ability to experience, enjoy and grow their own emotional life. In our current system the child who suffers such deep anguish and pain quietly will not get access to the support they need. They will never push themselves forward and they will not be easy to approbate and return your joy in learning. "Joy" is an affect that is very hard for children who have suffered trauma to experience.

It is up to the adults around that child, namely the carers, the adoptive parents, the teacher and the TA, to identify that need and put the support in place to help the child achieve their full potential; it is our duty to do so. A school with a sound emotional intelligent supportive ethos, which recognises and nurtures the emotional and social needs of the child, can deeply affect the future potential of damaged children to have a fulfilled experience of life:

> "Our adopted daughter did present a lot of problems for the teachers; she had post-traumatic stress disorder and was in a state of fear most of the time. She would never sit still, she found it hard to concentrate, she would get panic attacks a lot of the time and not be able to do anything, she took a lot of the

TA's time. If she was in what she perceived as a threatening situation she could explode, and on two occasions did; she behaved in unpredictable ways in the classroom. We were incredibly well supported by the school who had an open door for us as parents if we were worried, which was most of the time. When issues arose they held her very well and dealt with any behavioural problems with other children swiftly. The TA, who had experience of fostering and adopting, stayed with her throughout her time in the school and has become part of our family. The teachers took time to get to know her and make her feel safe; they tried setting up friendship groups for her which weren't successful, but we knew they were trying to help her socialise. We feel that the support and social world of the school helped her believe in herself because she was important to them and she knew they believed in her. Educationally she is very needy but her experience at school was bringing her into the social world. It has taken time but she's safe enough now, at secondary school, to begin to open herself up to learning. The school was incredibly important to her emotional and social development; the change in her over the years she was there was incredible, you could see this lovely person emerge into the world, and we owe all the staff a great deal."

Adopters (2010)

Teacher "avoidance"

It is essential that teachers know about a traumatised child's background if they are to teach them safely. However uncomfortable you may feel about knowing details of the abuse or neglect, you must put the needs of the children first. You will need only to know what is appropriate, and most adopters and foster carers will want you to have an idea of what the child has been through while protecting the child's right to confidentiality. It is crucial that you get as clear a picture as possible of what may frighten them and what makes them feel safe. Take time to get to know them and let them know that you understand that they may get scared. You will need to work closely with the parents to build continuity and paths to safety for them. You can work with the child to implement ways in which they can let you know when they are in trouble. Not all children will be able to do this when they have a trigger moment or a panic attack but some may be able to build up to it (see Chapter 8 on the feelings square). The fact that you show understanding and are supporting the child gives them the knowledge that the adult they are with is supporting and caring. You will also begin to recognise behaviours and physical signs such as when a trigger occurs and the child is moving into hyper-arousal. The following comes from the carer of a girl aged seven who had suffered extreme emotional and physical abuse up to the age of five:

"When we spoke about our 7-year-old daughter to her teachers when she moved into a new year group we found that the male teachers were less able to let us talk about her history. One said 'I don't need to know about that', although we insisted and gave him an overview of her background and fears. His problem with listening to the information made it difficult for us [. . .] you only want to keep your child safe. Later that term he showed a film in the classroom and turned the lights off so the school-room became very dark. Our daughter crawled along the floor to get to the light coming through the door and was asked to move back to her place. No one understood she was terrified of the lights going off and being in the dark. The effect on her was to trigger feelings of terror and she was very shaky after that; her nightmares came back. When we told her teacher about this he was very sorry and said that he'd wanted to make the experience of watching the film more dramatic for everyone. Teachers need to know that closing blinds and putting our children in the dark is very frightening for them. When we trained as fosters carers we were told to be careful around such things as closing curtains or blinds – actions that might have happened before the child was abused. I don't think we had talked about her being frightened of the dark, we didn't think she'd be put in that situation in the classroom. Why aren't teachers trained in understanding children suffering from post-traumatic stress disorder? Our daughter went through another abusive experience in school that day and it made us very angry."

Carer (2009)

Controlling behaviour

Teachers must be very careful about how they contain or set boundaries on a child's behaviour who has suffered from trauma and damaged development. We discussed "disintegrative shame" in Chapter 1 of this book regarding the pattern in a child's development when the prime giver shames the child, breaking attunement, but does not re-attune and integrate the feeling of shame. The sense of shame overwhelms the child who cannot then regulate their feelings of stress, anger or rage. When we chastise a child for their behaviour we are breaking the attunement we have with that child in our teacher–pupil relationship. This moment of being "told off" is difficult for any child because it revisits the powerful feeling of shame (the most uncomfortable affect). But the reaction of a child who is already overwhelmed by shame will be one, some, or all of the following:

- To damage any attachment or attunement you are building with the child.
- To reaffirm the child's sense of worthlessness (all adults shame and reject me).
- Trigger feelings of shame and send the child into hyper-arousal: possible anger and rage.
- Trigger feelings of shame and send the child into dissociation, i.e. freezing and not moving or answering. Sometimes perceived as "dumb insolence" by the teacher but in reality the child is in an extreme state of dissociation. The feeling of danger you have created by chastising them is so great that they can do nothing.

The teacher may see the behaviour as the child fulfilling their belief that they are badly behaved and wanting to challenge the teacher's authority, but it may be an uncontrollable reaction to a stimulus that activates their intense, overwhelming feeling of shame.

I remember a boy in my school, who was caned by the teacher for his bad behaviour, standing silent and staring in front of him, unable to apologise to a child he had hurt. The boy came from a violent family background. I am inclined, now, to believe that he was not goading the teacher but was in a state of frozen terror.

How then do we set consequences for inappropriate or unacceptable behaviours with vulnerable children?

Behaviour consequences – pre-empting situations

Pre-empt the situation before it occurs, because it will happen, since the child cannot control their inner tensions and anguish indefinitely. They cannot regulate themselves physiologically.

- Negotiate with the child separately so that they know what you expect of them and what will happen if they cannot sustain the level of behaviour you need to run the class.
- Negotiate with them as a team. You are working it out together.
- Show you understand that they have trouble controlling their behaviour and work through the Feelings Square (Chapter 8).
- Try to attune to them and show belief in them. Sit opposite them and mirror their movements; smile and be calm, positive and supportive. Try to gain eye contact.
- Accept that they may have moments when they cannot contain their worries and carry out the consequence to *help* them *regulate* their behaviour.
- Use the word "regulate" and explain it to the child by drawing a thermometer or a volcano with them and showing the degree of heat (anger/worry/wobbly feelings) increasing. Let the child know that there is language for and an understanding of his or her behaviour; other children have this issue and they are not alone. Grown-ups understand. Use the drawing of the object to help you explain. The child is likely to share more with you if they can be involved with another activity.
- The consequence for the behaviour may involve the child leaving the class. If so, use a phrase such as "downtime John" or "quiet five minutes Molly" so that the TA and the child know what is required of them and they can leave the situation without too much focus on them which will exacerbate their feelings of shame and anger.
- Try and spot the behaviour early. You may see the physical signs of hyper-vigilance leading to hyper-arousal or the child may have a pattern of movements that you or your TA may begin to recognise.

■ The "consequence" is not punishment – it is helping them be the boss of their behaviour (use their metaphor for this if you wish).

■ *Reintegrate the child back into the classroom when they return.* This is essential to break the pattern of shame and loss of attunement. When they re-enter the classroom smile at them and find a moment to go over and say, "Well done John, you're the boss." Reaffirm the attunement. You like them but you don't like their behaviour.

The issues for traumatised children are manifold, and every child will be unique in the way they experience and manifest their trauma.

Teacher empathy is the most valued teacher quality cited by pupils. They become effective teachers because they give time to the student beyond the classroom context.

(Braithwaite 1989)

4

Experiential Drama

Drama – Related to the Greek verb *dran-* "to do".

Drama is a Greek word meaning "action". Drama is about doing something – when we are "in action" something happens and we experience it.

We have seen how emotional knowledge is developed in children. You now have an insight into the process and how the brain is hard-wired to make emotional responses first and reasoned responses second.

You are now able to make your classroom a safe place where children can be open to learning. You know how to use your skills and personality to create class rapport and a one-to-one rapport that is within your comfort zone, allowing control, calmness and an openness to learning in your pupils. You are aware of how to use your teaching style and the way your pupils learn. You have greater insights into yourself and your pupils' strengths and needs.

Now it is time to look at integrating experiential drama into your practice.

We aren't talking about acting

Forget "acting" – we aren't talking about acting in the context of performance, techniques or rehearsal. You and the children are not going to be expected to act.

Drama for teaching is an extension of your imaginative approach to engage, connect and sustain the learning experience for the child. You will be heightening your imaginative approach to teaching. You are entering the learning from a different position by tapping into the child's imagination.

Think of "play"

Imagine a young child putting shapes into a shoebox which a parent or carer has made. They place the shapes into a little slot in the box over and over again.

The repetition, the feel of the box, the placing of the shape, the sound of the "plop" when the shape hits the bottom of the box, all go into the massive "C drive" of the child's brain as it computes the learning experience. Fine motor skills, colour, feel, sound, smell: the child is taking on the experience through the senses and is feeling pleasure at the task being completed. If the parent approbates the child's success with an animated voice, a smiling face, clapping, the child responds, follows the model of behaviour the parent or carer is providing and copies that behaviour. Smiling and clapping happily, the child sets off to repeat the task.

Think of the toddler wobbling around in its mother's shoes, following her as she vacuums the house, with a toy vacuum cleaner mirroring her actions. The mother approbates her little helper as they set about their task together. The child learns through play, through watching, mirroring and trying out the experience. Imitating, experiencing and experimenting. We call this playing but it is the child learning, printing the behaviour it experiences in its world.

Playing to learn is an interesting ethos to take into the classroom. Drama or action allows us to play and experience other lives and situations safely in a learning environment.

What we retain when learning

- What we read: 10 per cent
- What we hear: 20 per cent
- What we see: 30 per cent
- What we see and hear: 50 per cent
- What we are shown/explained/experience (see/hear/say/do) 90 per cent.

When teaching, you are 90 per cent knowledgeable regarding your understanding of the subject, but how are you delivering your knowledge to the children? How much is the child receiving, learning and remembering? If you want to develop their empathy and ability to connect to learning how will you facilitate this connection through the way you teach?

Let us look at how using experiential teaching can help you deliver to your children:

1. Help children engage with learning
2. Build imaginative capacity
3. Experience how to play
4. Experience learning through emotions, reasoning and reflection
5. Make sense of their lives and work through issues that worry them
6. Make sense of their own actions and the actions of others
7. Feel important – their opinions matter
8. Interact with each other socially in a safe environment

9. Learn social and emotional skills to take outside the classroom
10. Experiment safely with situations – testing boundaries
11. Learn group respect – group working
12. Make decisions and problem-solving
13. Experience positive situations and role models
14. Change perceptions and their patterned responses through experiential understanding.

Experiencing and integrating positional drama

Metaphors for emotional understanding

The use of metaphor is very powerful for emotional learning. Metaphor allows children to visit and make sense of situations and issues in a safe way. We can look at life through the window of someone else's experience.

When I was directing an adopted young people's project, the children devised a story to perform for their parents. Some of the children in the group had been recently placed with their adoptive families; others had been with their adoptive parents for a period of two to three years. The play the children devised was about a princess who lived in a castle. By day she walked with her cat in a beautiful garden, while by night a wicked ogre, who lived in the tower of her castle, would come and trample on all the flowers in her garden. She ran away from the castle but she was spotted by the orgre's spies who took her into a forest. A prince rescued her and took her to his parents who looked after them both. They returned to the princess' castle and the ogre was told off by everyone. At the end of the play the children lined up and each spoke to the ogre in turn, saying things like "Stop hurting people" or "Go away". One boy had joined in the games but was too agitated to take part in the devising process. He had been in the room drawing our "set" on flip chart pages with social workers who were supporting the project and he had decided to hold these pages up as a background to the action. At the end of the play I asked him if he wanted to say anything to the ogre. He marched up to the boy who was playing the ogre and said, "Be kind!" The play the children devised describes a safe garden being destroyed after dark by a dangerous creature. The girl escapes, but spies take her into a dangerous forest. A prince rescues her and takes her to a safe place where there are kind adults. The adults, the prince and princess return to the ogre and are empowered to face him and have a voice. The play, of their own making, is a metaphor for their stories. In making the story and experiencing it they act out a different ending where they return to the ogre and tell him off. Even though their retribution in the soft language of the little boy is "Be kind!" they are giving themselves power in their situation.

Daniel Golman talks about the game of "Purdy" where, in an elementary school playground in California in 1989, the children re-enacted a real event where a gunman (Patrick Purdy) visited the playground and fired a submachine-gun into the crowds of hundreds of children before killing himself. Five children died and twenty-nine were wounded. Many of the children suffered from post traumatic stress following the event as well as hyper-vigilance. Many would not go out into the playground again or became fearful of sirens and loud bangs.

Following the shooting, the children started to play a game in the playground called "Purdy". The villain fires a gun at the children and kills them and then kills himself, or he fires at the children but they kill him. The children begin to play the game and change the outcome of the traumatic event. The repeated playing of the game helps them to try to make sense of the terrible event they have witnessed and that has printed itself in their memories, and to work through the resulting trauma. They relive the trauma safely at play. It enables the participants to desensitise the event and allows a set of non-traumatised senses to become associated with it. Changing the ending empowers them to be less fearful by giving them mastery over the traumatic event (Golman 1996). We may recognise similar behaviours in children who have gone through a difficult experience in hospital or at a funeral of a family member and who repeat the event in play: they are working through what they have experienced and trying to understand it. Games and play allow children to distance themselves from events and experiences.

The adopted children's group used a fairy-tale framework to revisit their traumatic background and empower themselves,while the traumatised children in California created a game that allowed them to revisit the trauma, and to control and change it.

Working out life through experiential play is part of our emotional survival equipment.

5

Positional Drama

Definition of *Position*:
To put in the proper or appropriate place. To put someone or something in a position, especially in relation to others. A fact or a viewpoint.

When we experience or make a decision about anything we do it from our own viewpoint. Our point of view is dependent upon our life experiences and our social and cultural backgrounds, as is our pupils'. We are biased, since we see a situation from our point of view. Children will often look to adults to signal what their point of view or reaction to a situation should be. Initially children will look to their parents or carers, but as they move into the outside world their reactions will be shaped by other significant adults. Many is the parent who, when in the midst of correcting behaviour or pointing out a fact, will be told by their child, "Oh no that's not right because teacher says [. . .]". If the teacher can facilitate the child to step into another person's shoes and experience other people's points of view then we are developing a process of understanding and empathy that the child will be able to use as a learning and life tool. We want the children to ask the question, "Why did/does that person do that? Why do they think differently from me?" And then we want them to analyse and understand why, and to see that there were other options which that person could have taken.

Another pair of shoes

When I was directing a devising drama project in a museum that had once been the concentration camp in Stutthoff,[1] just outside Gdansk in Poland I worked with young people and educators from Poland, Germany and America. The group members were not sure of each other when we began the work. As we walked to the museum and saw the wooden barracks through the rusty wire a Polish student told me her grandparents had died in the camp and that, as a consequence, she was concerned about her feelings in the group as she "didn't

FIGURE 5.1 The Ripples Project – Teatr Wybrzeze and the Stutthof Musuem in Sztutowo, Gdansk, Poland. Students from Poland and America

like Germans". On one of our workshop days I placed a pair of children's shoes on the floor of our rehearsal room. We talked about the shoes and who they might have belonged to at that time. We had seen a hut full of shoes, and the lost lives and personalities that seemed to be held in the fading pieces of coloured leather evoked very powerful feelings in all of us. Our pair of shoes became a starting point – they created a history of a young girl to whom they had belonged. The group began filling those shoes with her life. Two of the group became the child and told her story; others became people around her life. Each saw her in a different way, from a different social and emotional point of view. We built many people from objects and from actual letters to which we had access in the archives. We experienced, at a safe distance, the misery, the pain and the exulta-tion of a survivor who spoke to us about surviving the camp and, following liberation, returning to his mother's house on his birthday.[2] The German and Polish students worked closely with each other throughout the process and became friends. The experience of building the stories through history (letters and research), place and imagination changed our perceptions of each other, the war and the future. As one of the German students said to me, "I thought that doing this would help me be able to leave it behind me. I know now I can never leave it behind me."

When we work with children on positional drama our aim is to place them in another pair of shoes – the metaphor for another life, another person, another set of social circumstances, possibly another historical time. The children are facilitated to understand and empathise with this new person and to try and see the world from their experience and through their eyes.

The model permits children to experience other people, other lives and other times, and to create and learn through that experience. It allows the children to create characters and stories imaginatively, to study extant stories, to experience history in an experiential and exciting way, and to explore PSHE issues of life and behaviour in a safe way. The entire model drives through an engagement in the learning through ownership, emotional connection and imagination.

The full model is a framework for structured, experiential learning. The rules are that you develop the skill of giving the children ownership of the work and, when you assume the "positions" as characters you *stay* with the position and point of view you have created, and shape the work from the perspective and thoughts of the character you are serving. It can be as simple or as complex as the subject and class needs you are teaching. It can be used from Reception onward. The teacher tempers the length and level of delivery to suit the situation.

A subject for exploration is identified. This may be:

- For PSHE issues such as bullying and exploring behaviours
- For creative writing, building characters, story, structure and vocabulary
- For exploring books you are studying
- For studying and engaging with history
- You can apply aspects of the model to facilitate creative research in other subjects (e.g. religious education or geography).

When using positional drama you are facilitating your class to work as a collective to create believable three-dimensional people, places and situations, and the children build on each other's ideas. There is a firm structure to the creative process which is controlled by the teacher. You are helping them to understand people, what motivates them and the world they inhabit, and to expand their understanding and empathy.

In the issue-based model you are helping the children to understand themselves and each other and to question behaviours. In the writing model you are helping them to see that writing needs to be structured and planned. Character, place and situation need to be imagined or drawn from life's experience, and then extended and developed in detail to build a good story. You then reflect on what you have made prior to everyone writing. The linguistic logical approach of talking about a situation or character and suggesting a first line or paragraph, even a strong, dramatic one, will not scaffold a child who is strongly kinaesthetic or visual towards creating and sustaining writing a story. You must use the techniques of facilitating an emotional and imaginative visual and kinaesthetic connection to the subject that will give children frameworks upon which to build.

As the children become familiar with the process you will be able to use single stages of the model to work in specific subject areas. The model is incredibly flexible. It may be used in an afternoon or as a model for a themed piece of work over a much longer period. It may be split into sections which you are able to extract and utilise when you are working in certain areas (e.g. studying historical characters or characters from literature, creating characters, looking at environments in historical contexts, or looking at why writers choose to set their work in specific times and places). Once the children understand the process you can, literally, mix and match elements of it to suit your needs.

The emphasis on time spent at each of the six stages changes between the creative writing model, the history model and the issue-based PSHE model. This is because you will be building characters on creative imagination, historical fact, research resources, and imagination and behavioural issues respectively.

One teacher delivering experiential learning in a school will have a positive socialising and learning effect upon the pupils in his or her class, building up their resilience and emotional intelligence. A whole school ethos of experiential delivery where teachers share and develop their practice will have an even greater social and learning impact. This is done primarily via the headteacher's engagement and drive, but also through the teachers socialising and sharing the practice and development of ideas and working cooperatively as a team.

The Positional Drama model outline

The stages of positional drama are explained below and specific models outlined so that you can see their potential and use them as a template for your own work.

The stages are as follows:

1. *Catalyst*: Engaging the children with the theme or character using a catalyst.
2. *Building characters*: Building the central character and then building secondary characters'age/gender/characteristics /time/ social world and background.
3. *Creating the place*: Deciding where the action will be set and creating it.
4. *Building the situation*: Making a situation that uses the characters you have made to further an understanding of study area (writing, literature study, history, issues).
5. *Entering the situation*: Assuming positions and understanding character and situations from different viewpoints.
6. *Reflecting: on the process, discussing and drawing conclusions*, using the resource you have created in the process for writing.

The model offers a simple formula for creating and structuring a story, studying history, studying literature or exploring issues by building characters, place and situation in a three-dimensional way.

THE CENTRAL CHARACTER: Who they are, what they like and dislike, their family, feelings and background. *Secondary characters* – either created specifically for the story or people who have been built around the original character.

PLACE: Where the characters are physically in the story.

SITUATION: The circumstances in which the characters find themselves.

ACTION: What happens in the situation.

ENTERING THE SITUATION: Experiencing and experimenting with the situation and its possible outcomes.

REFLECTING/CONCLUSION: Discussing options and deciding which outcomes work best for the story.

The work is character led. This is to make it focused and experiential for the children. It is easier for a child to create and engage with a character than to create and engage with a story or situation. With this model they are led through the wider process motivated by the characters they have created.

Here are four templates to explain the model and how it may be used for:

1. History
2. Creative writing
3. Understanding characters you are reading in literature
4. Issue-based work for PSHE and SEAL.

Each template is a complete model for you to use, so there may be some repetition regarding the model.

Stage 1 Catalyst

The teacher facilitates the building of this person so that the children have a strong sense of his or her character. This is achieved, initially, through a catalyst which engages the children's interest and imagination. You may word-scape the catalyst to squeeze as many ideas from it as possible (for word-scapes see Chapter 7). The character is given a context regarding historical period and social background. In the initial stage we show the children the character and engage them in the character's development. The catalyst can also feed into the construction of the situation (Stage 4). For example, if the catalyst is a Roman soldier's helmet the situation may take place in a soldiers' barracks; if it is a

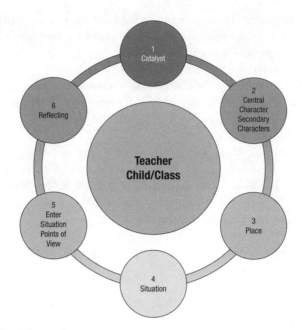

FIGURE 5.2 Positional drama stages

gas-mask the situation may take place in a London underground station during the Blitz in the Second World War.

Stage 2 Central character

The teacher draws an outline of the character on the whiteboard and begins to build a literal and psychological picture of the person. We decide their age, appearance friends, family, interests, aspirations or lack of them, and so on. The teacher keeps the children on track and does not allow them to digress into easy, one-dimensional options.

It is essential to challenge thinking especially if the children contradict each other or if one child becomes too enthusiastic and wants to create the person alone. An important part of the social aspect of the drama is to make the children listen to each other's offers and build on them together. Approbate all offers, even those you do not accept. The teacher must facilitate the children's sense of ownership through this process. They will be building the person from their experience and understanding of the world. Once the children feel that they know and understand the character they will be able to empathise and engage with the character in a specific situation. The character becomes a safe extension of the child that they can then work through in the process.

Secondary characters

You will find that your central characters will be surrounded by other people who are important to them. You can take one or two of these secondary characters and build on them (e.g. in the history template you will need to create a foreman in the mill; in the bullying template you will need to create the bully's mother and the child who is bullied). You will have secondary characters that will be necessary for your situation and they will need to be built now in the same way in which you have built your central character.

Stage 3 Place

Next you have to create the place where the action of your situation will happen. If your work is historical you will look at a place that is in a specific period with a specific social structure (e.g. Tudor, Victorian or Second World War). If you are creating a place for your own stories you may need to research different countries or create something that is based in imagination and fantasy. You may need to research, sound-scape or word-scape these places (see Chapter 7).

Stage 4 Situation

Once you have your characters you will need to place them in a situation. How you facilitate the structure of the situation will be led by your initial catalyst and the characters you have created. The creation of the situation may be either teacher or pupil led. It is important that the situation should contain a conflict. This will help the later construction of the scene – it needs a tension between the characters. It is always desirable to have a fail-safe situation to fall back upon; you may never need it but it will give you confidence to know it is there.

When you are using positional drama for creative writing you may want to let the children offer possible situations and discuss their differing potential regarding the scope for strong story-telling. This will build the children's understanding of how conflict, time and place are crucial to creative writing.

For issue-based work it is likely that you will have a specific situation in which to place your characters that will focus on the issues you want to explore. You still need to offer this in a way that will engage the children, and to tie the situation into the catalyst is a good way to accomplish this, as the children will have drawn their character/s from it.

Stage 5 Entering the situation

Once the situation has been agreed upon the central character is placed into it with one of the other characters and they improvise using their character outlines. You may create a brief for the situation where characters must do, ask or find out something. This will help the children who enter the situation interact with each other.

Initially, the improvisation can be short with feedback from the other children who are watching. This process continues until we have a scene. Another character can then be placed into the scene as required to further the story. You may want to create more than one scene. Once the scene is created, other children can enter it and experience playing the characters. When the children give feedback it must be from their point of view. If someone is in the character of a child they cannot say what the parent is thinking; only what they are thinking and feeling. You may want to team up the characters so that the children watching must support one character, whether that is the child mill worker who is being abused by the mill system, or the foreman who must get her to keep working. The children must experience being in another character's "shoes" whether they agree with that character or not. Gaining another perspective widens the child's perspective and understanding.

The rules are as follows:

1. The children must adhere to the brief that has been mapped out by the class.
2. Children playing characters *must* stay with that character's point of view at all times and be true to the person they have created in stages 1 and 2 of the process.
3. Children playing characters describe what motivates their actions, and how their character feels.
4. Character actions and feelings may be "thought-tracked" by children not taking part in the scene and then agreed upon as right for that character.
5. The scene is scripted on whiteboard (or filmed) for feedback.

At this stage you are working as a team, analysing and building on the work in progress.

Are the characters true to what you have created and is their behaviour believable in their situation? As the teacher, you will need to challenge children who want to use tricks or "magic" to change situations. You must keep the children on track with the truth of what you are making. If there are historical constructs, stick to them (e.g. the mill girl cannot walk out of her job because she will probably starve if she does). This will make history very real for the participants. You cannot force a bully to say "sorry" and stop bullying because you want him or her to do so – you must find the truth of the situation. If you are creating a fantasy story, then, of course, magic is allowed.

Stage 6 Reflecting

The scene or scenes are discussed by the group. If you are using positional drama to create characters and scenarios for creative writing you will be reflecting on the character. The same process is followed if you are exploring a written character in a book.

1. Was the character well drawn?
2. Did you believe in him or her?
3. Was the place you created for the action strong? Why was it strong?
4. Why is place important in a story?
5. Was there another place that would have been as strong?

6. Why did the characters function in the way they did in the situation?
7. How did the characters feel?
8. How did we think the characters felt – was it different?
9. What did we learn about the characters through the situation?
10. What could the next situation be?

Discuss the strength of your process of creating character, place and action to build the children's understanding of the importance of character, place and dynamic tension in a story.

If you are using positional drama for history you will be reflecting on the period, social circumstances and whether the characters are functioning as they would have done at that time. You can reflect on the restrictions of different times on the life and freedom of children, adults and different social classes.

Once you have reflected on the work you have made together you can move into written work. Here are some ideas:

1. Write out the story of the work you have created, describing the characters and place. Write the story from one character's point of view. Groups of children can take different characters and write the story from their point of view (e.g. the dragon and the knight in the quest template will give very different accounts of the same story). This will show the children how you can shift points of view in writing to give different slants on the same tale.
2. Write a poem about the place you have created.
3. Write out the thoughts of the main character.
4. Write the story as a script.
5. Story board the story, making more situations and building towards a conclusion.

Positional drama allows children to own and build work as a team with your guidance. It helps them understand the creation of characters – interaction – making a strong place for the stories' action to happen in – and a situation that holds tension/conflict and excitement. By the end of a session they should have enough of a structure on which to hang their own writing work.

Positional drama: history template

In the positional drama history model you may either pre-research the period and area you will be working in so that you build a body of information with the children and then use the model to bring it to life, or use the catalyst stage to introduce the subject and motivate the children to research it. The children then experience the history in a very real way. You will facilitate the children to give you ideas; you can accept offers of their ideas and either let them lead the character work, or you can make suggestions or give the characters that they develop creatively and own.

You will need to set the level of control of the creative process regarding the historical characters you will build, the place they inhabit and the situation they are in. Some teachers will want to lead or set the model stages and others will be happy to let the children lead in certain areas. Always work well within your comfort zone and experiment with your facilitation of the children's creativity as you develop your technique and confidence with the model.

Stage 1 Engaging catalyst

In the initial stage we are engaging the children with the character they are creating and we achieve this in an exciting and imaginative way through a catalyst. The children become investigators who need to study the catalyst and discover who it may belong to – you can make this either simple or challenging.

Seat the children in a circle where the catalyst object can initially be placed in the centre and studied by all, and then passed around for closer examination. The teacher uses the catalyst to facilitate the creation of this person so that the children can have a strong sense of his or her character. The catalyst can also feed into the Stage 3 "Place" element of the model. For example, if the catalyst is a Roman soldier's helmet the situation may take place in a soldier's barracks, at the Roman Baths, watching a chariot race or playing dice while guarding Jesus on the cross; the children will give you many options.

You may want to study a historical character such as Elizabeth I, Queen Boadicea, Guy Fawkes, Mary Seacole or Henry VIII. In this case you may use the catalyst of Elizabeth's pomander, copies of Guy Fawkes' signature before and after he was tortured in the tower or a green hat respectively. In our model we are looking at a Victorian girl who works in a mill. Our catalyst could be:

- Victorian money (sixpence or penny with Queen Victoria's head on it)
- A piece of cotton cloth
- A dirty pinafore
- A piece of embroidery
- Rough cotton from a loom
- A teasel
- A large cut sandwich wrapped in cloth
- A combination of these items (e.g. cloth and penny).

You can lead on this by saying that you know the person comes from Victorian times and that they don't seem to have a lot of money. The children may well offer this to you if you have researched this period with them. Approbate whatever offers they accept and build towards the character you want the children to create. A cap or an apron allows them to create a boy or a girl you choose which you want for the work. Build up the catalyst entrance into the group: "I have a very interesting object here that is going to help us discover/create/meet a person from the past. Let's see if we can work out who it belonged to."

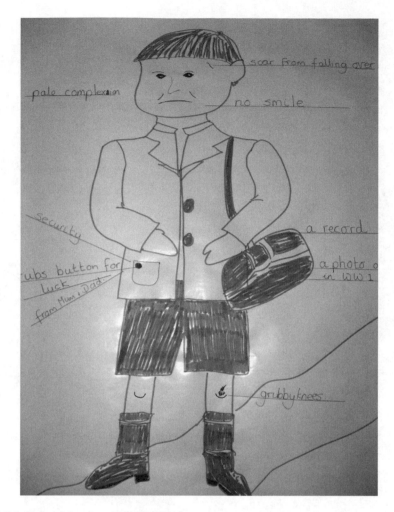

FIGURE 5.3 Photo of drawing of Billy the Evacuee

You place the Victorian penny (it may become part of the story) in the middle of your circle and let the children discuss it. This will help clarify the period in which you are setting the piece and you may ask, "Who do you think owns this?" If you want to lead them more in the question ask, "Who was the young girl who owned this penny? It was lot of money to her." Remember: you can manipulate a great deal by the way you introduce the catalyst or you can place more than one item into the circle so that the children can follow a trail of clues to the person, or each one can build another element of the character. You will usually find that two items will give the children a strong sense of who they are "meeting" through this process. By the end of the catalyst stage you will have engaged the children and decided on the character you will create together. In the history model you will want to incorporate as many facts as possible.

The catalyst has led you towards a character – you are ready to move on to the next stage.

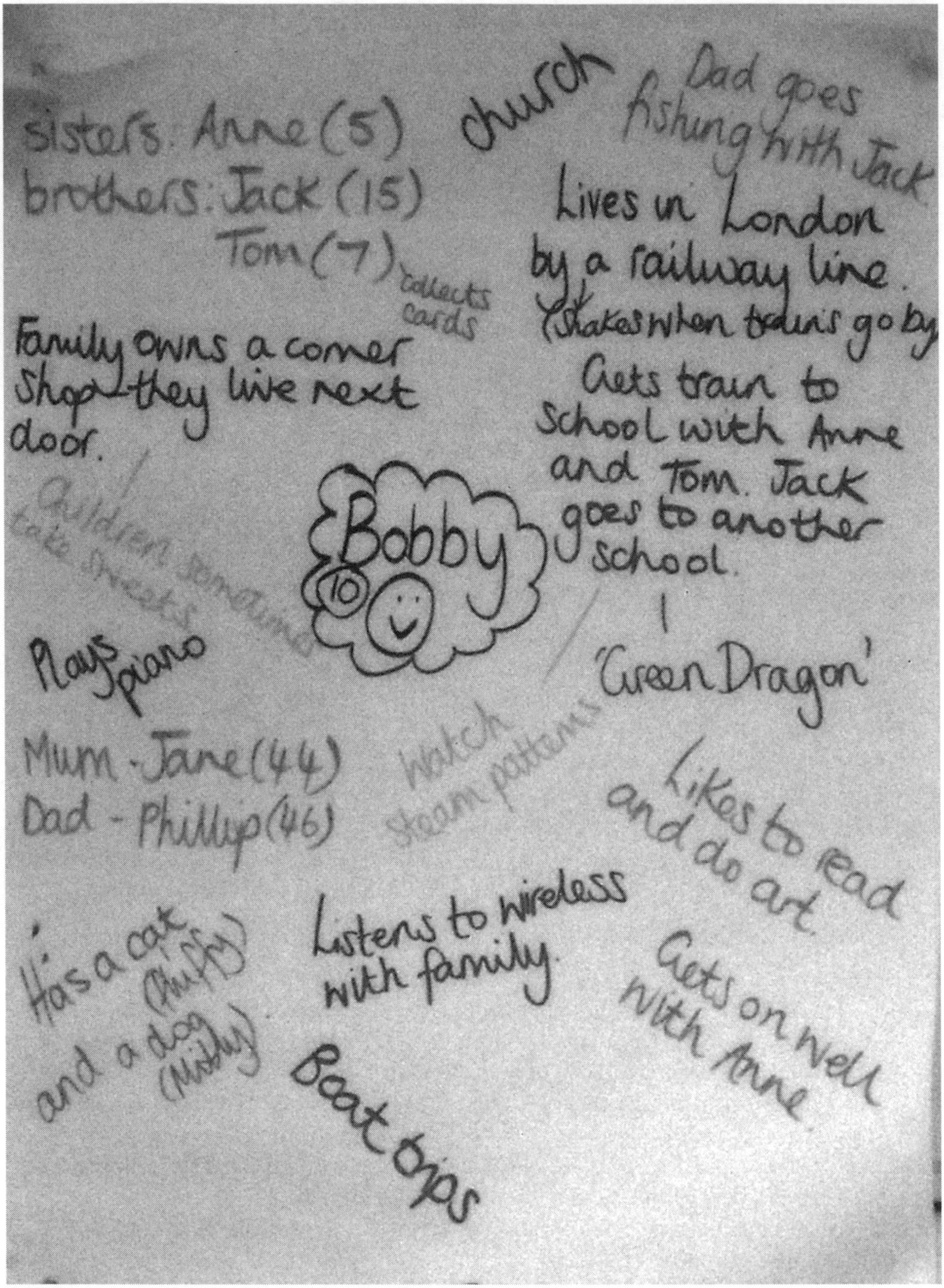

sisters: Anne (5)
brothers: Jack (15)
Tom (7) collects cards

church
Dad goes fishing with Jack
Lives in London by a railway line. Shakes when trains go by
Gets train to school with Anne and Tom. Jack goes to another school.

Family owns a corner shop—they live next door.

Children sending take sweets

Bobby 10

'Green Dragon'

Plays piano

Mum - Jane (44)
Dad - Phillip (46)

Watch steam patterns

Likes to read and do art.

Has a cat (Puffy) and a dog (Misty)

Listens to wireless with family.

Gets on well with Anne

Boat trips

FIGURE 5.4 Building a character in words: Bobby the Evacuee by Years 5 and 6 studying the Second World War

Stage 2 Central and secondary characters

Central character

The character is given a context:

1. Age, gender and name: a girl, aged 12, called Lilly Dorking
2. Historical period: Victorian
3. Place: Lancashire
4. Social background: a poor mill worker.

The teacher then draws an outline of the person on the whiteboard. The outline needs to be quite large, as you will be writing and possibly drawing on it to help to build a literal and psychological picture of the person. The children help decide their gender, age, appearance, what they do, their likes and dislikes, where they live, friends, family, and so on. If they offer a friend, parent or sibling draw the outline and write the name in it and say you may work on that person later. You must complete the central character before working on the others.

It is essential to challenge thinking, especially if the children contradict each other, or get them to decide which idea they want to use, or put both up on the board. If one child becomes too enthusiastic and wants to create the person alone you must make it clear that this is a team effort and everyone must have a chance to have their ideas heard. In one school the teacher used the term "give way – another idea's coming" and the children took this as their shorthand signal to allow others to speak.

An important part of the social aspect of the drama is for the children to listen to each other's offers and build on them together. Approbate all offers, even those you do not take; this encourages everyone to feel they can take part. A refusal of an offer can be damaging to a child's sense of their importance to you in the creative situation. The teacher must facilitate the children's strong sense of ownership throughout the process. They will be building the person from their experience and understanding of the world and, with your support, extending this into the historical context. Once the children feel that they know and understand the character they will be able to empathise and engage with the character in a specific situation. The character becomes a safe extension of the children that they can then work through in the process. They will talk about how Lilly or the foreman or her brother feels and whether life was fair to them in Victorian times, but they will also be able to understand and apply it to their own experiences.

Secondary characters

There will be other characters that you will want to build into your situation and they are created in the same way as the central character. You will take them from the people identified as being important to the character in the first stage. You can either let the children decide which of these characters you will build on and take into the situation or you can make the decision yourself.

FIGURE 5.5 Teacher leading Stage 2: Creating characters

You may have planted this character in the first stage or you may directly give them one now who you say Lilly knows. For example, the children may have created a brother for Lilly who works with her in the mill. You will decide to build on this and add the mill foreman and build him up as well. When you use positional drama for the first time keep your secondary characters to a minimum so that you maintain your impetus and focus. As you progress and feel more confident you may spread the model over a longer period of time in researching and developing your characters; you may build up more people who work in the mill, or the mill manager who has more social standing, or you may get Lord Shaftsbury to visit the mill and look at the working conditions of children. As long as the model engages the children in the learning it is useful to you.

Stage 3 Place

Once you have your characters you will need to identify the place or setting they are in. This is important for your situation. We can place the mill girl in her small home – a cottage or tiny house shared with others – on a hillside overlooking the village/town/mill or in the mill itself amidst the heat, danger and relentless noise of her work environment. If you are thinking ahead to a dramatic situation you may ask the children to offer you places and then suggest that the mill offers the best dramatic situation. *You* can also set the place and ask them to build up what they feel it is like.

This place will have a historical and social context that is appropriate to your characters. For example, if you have been working on building a female woollen mill worker her "place" will be as follows:

> *Period*: Victorian times, c. 1875
>
> *Social situation*: Working class, very poor but earning (not in the workhouse)
>
> *Place*: In the cotton mill.

You can send the children off to research the cotton mills, what they looked like, working conditions, rates of pay and the jobs children would do. You could draw on history resources such as photographs or paintings to build a clear feel for the place. This may mean that you will spend more time building this stage. When you have a strong idea of place with your class it is always valuable to sound-scape and word-scape the place. You can use the machine workshop idea and create the noises of the mill machines. The clog dances that the mill men and women developed used the rhythms of the shuttles and looms and steps were named after them. This will give you a wide cultural area to study regarding how the mill shaped the lives of the people both within and outside it.

Stage 4 Situation building

Once you have your characters and place you can create the situation that occurs there. How you facilitate the structure of the situation will be led by your characters and the place you have made. The creation of the situation may be either teacher or pupil led. The situation is often led by the teacher, as it is pivotal to the learning, but it is always valuable to let the children make offers, since these can be incorporated into your overview. They will often be very close to your thinking, especially if the other stages are shaped well. (When you are comfortable with the model you may want to work on more than one situation

FIGURE 5.6 Children creating and experiencing "place" space as workers resting

with different groups.) It is always desirable to have a fail-safe situation to fall back upon, you may never need it but it will give you confidence to know it is there.

Whether you are leading or facilitating, it is important that the situation should contain a conflict. This will help the building of the work later – it needs a tension between the characters.

If we continue with the female mill worker scenario her situation may be as follows.

An accident occurs on the looms as a result of the manager's refusal to install safety guards on the machinery. The other characters might be the girl's friend and the factory foreman. The children might add that the person who has been hurt is the girl's brother in order to heighten the tension, or the teacher may decide to add this element if it is felt to be appropriate. You write up the main points of what will be required in the scene and the characters must achieve this in the situation.

Stage 5 Entering the situation

Once the situation is agreed upon the central character is placed into it. One of the other characters is placed with the central character and they improvise around the situation, using their character outlines and the brief that has been given to them. Initially the improvisation can be short with feedback from the audience. This process continues until you have a scene. Another character may be placed into the scene as required to progress the story. Once the scene is made other children can enter it and experience playing the characters. The children watch the characters build up the scene.

1. The scene is discussed by the group and ideas to expand it are put into it.
2. Children playing the characters *must* stay with that character's point of view at all times.
3. Children playing the characters describe what motivates their actions, how they feel and so on.
4. Other children can go into the scene and play the characters – keeping to what has been built so far.
5. Character actions and feelings can be "thought-tracked" by other children not in the scene and then agreed upon as right for that character. The scene is scripted on the whiteboard (or recorded) for feedback. You may want to create more than one scene or develop the existing scene.

In the mill scene the girl may attack the foreman for not looking after the machinery but the children must remember that if she does so she risks losing her job as she has very little power in the situation, and no union to back her up. Losing her job may mean starvation and the workhouse. You would have researched the period so the children would be building their situation in the context of your shared knowledge. This lifts their understanding of the historical injustice of the times. The teacher must compel them to be true to the children of that period – this raises many points for discussion. It becomes a powerful insight into experiencing another child's life.

Stage 6 Conclusion/reflecting

In the mill girl model the reflection will be on child labour, the powerlessness of children in the Victorian period, and the social structure that made it permissible for working-class children to be abused in this way.

1. Were the characters well drawn and true to their social standing?
2. Did you believe they were living in that period of history? Why?
3. Why did they function in the way they did in the situation?
4. What might happen next? Why?

As always, children will see this in the context of their own lives and injustices, and it may become an interesting platform for discussion. It can then lead into written work.

As you discuss and reflect upon the work you have created together you can shape it towards written work, i.e.:

- A meeting is called by the workers to discuss what they can do to make the factory safer. Meet the boss? Stop working/strike?
- A Victorian newspaper report of the incident
- The girl or boy, when they are old, writing or retelling the story and what happened next
- Further research on factory conditions then and now – what has changed?

You may want to look at the Positional Drama Studying Literature Model that uses Oliver Twist, since this is a great book to use when studying Victorian history in the context of conditions for children, social differences and Victorian life. You could run the model over a period of time, looking at characters' conditions and history, and setting up and researching different places and situations with the characters.

Positional drama: creative writing template

Always have a scribe to write up ideas that the children offer you. Your TA can write ideas on a whiteboard to be referred to as the process develops. Take time to build descriptive vocabulary for characters, place and situation.

Writing resource

These ideas become a resource for later written work where you can approbate children's ideas and incorporate them. For example: "Do you remember when

Carl suggested that the crystal could have belonged to an old washer-woman who is really a good witch in disguise? How do you think she could be useful to the next stage of your story?" Or simply suggest that they dip into their pool of character and situation ideas to progress their stories. This will help children who become blocked in their writing because they find it difficult to build situations. As you create more ideas cooperatively the children will begin to understand the way stories can be built and that it is possible to have more than one option as to what may happen from one situation to the next. When the options are placed on the whiteboard/flipchart they become a rich store of alternative ideas for children who become blocked in their work.

You may want to keep a class story, place and character book where these ideas are written down under themed headings. This will be the children's collective work and something they can refer to when they are writing. This will help children understand how writers continually note ideas and keep them for later, like tucking a sweet away so that you have a nice surprise when you find it nestling in your pocket.

Stage 1 Engaging catalyst

You have decided to create a character and a story for a themed piece of creative writing on "Quests". You will build this character as a team and you want it to be the hero of the written piece. You will lead this through language and your opening catalyst. Your language should suggest ideas and not be prescriptive; you want the children to own the character and feel that they have created it. You might say: "We are going to create a character for a story. This person can be male or female, very young or old, it's up to us, but I have a clue that might help us create this person. Here it is. [Reveal the object which is a crystal. Make this moment special and dramatic – the object is intended to engage their interest and imagination. It is therefore very important that you give this moment importance.] I'll pass it around the circle; let's not say anything. Just pass it around and when you are holding it open up your imagination and see what ideas come into it."

Sometimes you may want to lead the thinking by giving certain cues. This will not stop the children having ownership of the work as they will still be making lots of offers to you. If you want to look at the character of a hero you may lead the thinking by saying, "A young man in olden times is searching for this object. He is riding a magnificent horse and he is very brave. Who do you think he is?" (if you phrase the question in this way the children will probably offer you a knight). You can phrase your question to create a female warrior in the same way: "A young women, in ancient times, is searching for this object. She is very brave and wears a sword that was given to her by her grandfather." Girls have many powerful heroines now from Walt Disney's "Mulan" to "Hermione" in Harry Potter. You can encourage them to take on positive and strong role models. In this instance you are looking at creating a character who faces obstacles with resolve, bravery and resilience. If you can facilitate a strong entry into the belief in the experiential drama work the children will be able to imagine themselves succeeding in this role.

If you want to build a hero or a heroine you could use one of the following catalysts:

- A sword (possibly wound around with a scarf for a woman)
- A cup, glass or chalice
- A dagger
- A handkerchief that you tell the children was a lady's favour and was given to a knight (Who was the lady? Who was the knight?)
- A scroll (letter) asking a warrior to come to the aid of a castle under siege
- A bloodied bandage or piece of cloth (this was from a great battle when someone was hurt but survived. What battle? Who was hurt? By whom?)
- A drawing of a coat of arms with clues on it, i.e.: an eagle and a dragon (Who did it belong to? Was it stolen?)
- A cloak or a piece of beautiful clothing
- An old bag of coins (a payment for ransom?)
- A crystal (magical charm, needs to be discovered or delivered to someone)
- A picture or painting of a knight
- A picture or painting of a woman warrior.

Three-dimensional objects or written texts containing clues work best as catalysts. Paintings and pictures are good but they do not have the experiential impact of something you can hold, feel the texture of and smell – scent can be a strong aid when sprayed on to an object.

The teacher leads the discussion from the catalyst: "Who do *we*, team [encourage the class to work together], think this object belongs to?" or "Who do you think may be searching for this object?"

Set up the framework so that the child who is speaking has to be holding the object, thus ensuring that ideas are listened to. The more you heighten the stakes of the offers and hold them in a class ritual the stronger the impact will be upon the children to approach the work seriously.

In this model the children offer us a young knight who is searching for the crystal.

Stage 2 Central and secondary characters

Central character

The teacher then draws a basic outline of the knight on the whiteboard. It needs to be of a reasonable size, as you will be writing and possibly drawing on it to help to build a literal and psychological picture of the character. Ask questions that help make him real: detail is good. Children tend not to write detail because it takes great observation and imagination to do this (I have put further prompts for you in brackets, which you can use if the children are slow to make offers or to build on offers they have made):

- How old is he?
- What's his name?
- What does he look like? (Tall/short/hair colour and length/eye colour; take offers and build on them. Has he any scars from battles? A beard?)
- What emblem does he have on his shield?
- Where does he live? (England? France? Spain?)
- Who are his friends? (Past friends, other knights?)
- Has he got a family? (If they do not offer family that is fine)
- Who does he fight for? (The King? Queen? Himself?)
- What colour is his horse?
- What is his horse's name?

The teacher keeps the children on track and does not allow them to digress or make offers that obviously contradict what is being built. You must complete the central character before working on others.

When you have finished this part of the process you should have a well-drawn character with a history. Other characters mentioned as friends or enemies are named and/or drawn on the whiteboard and may be carried into the next stage to develop.

Secondary characters

Once you have identified the secondary characters you build them in the same way. For example, there may be a wizard who also wants the crystal or a clever dragon/witch who is hiding it. When you are building secondary characters you must keep an eye on your place and situation, as they will need to fit into both. Remember: you can decide beforehand who you want the secondary character/s to be and leave the children to create them.

In this model we will create a clever, evil dragon who has obtained the crystal by foul means. If required, you may use another catalyst to help build secondary characters or, if you feel the children are engaged and the ideas are flowing, just continue with questions similar to the following:

- What does the dragon look like? (You may write or draw this on the board around a dragon shape)
- Does he breathe fire? What does his breath smell like?
- Can he speak? (You will need him to be able to speak for the story, so work this in with the children. Make it magical – perhaps the crystal allows him to speak or the knight has a spell that allows him to hear the dragon)
- Does he have friends or co-dragons who may work with him?

- Does he work for anybody, perhaps a wizard, or is he in the power of an enemy?
- Where does he live?
- Where is he hiding the crystal?

Once you are satisfied that your character is complete you can lead into place. This could be hooked on to the last two questions, "Where does the dragon live?" and "Where is it hiding the crystal?" If the children offer two different places for this (i.e. a cave and a mountain-top) you or they can choose which is the best place to set your story.

Stage 3 Place

If the children suggest that the dragon lives in a cave you should give them options as to where the cave might be located, so they can see that there are always choices to be made, and that some choices offer more scope for writing than others. For example, the cave could be near the sea in a cliff face that the knight must climb to, by a magical lake, or deep underground in a maze of tunnels, or in a forest. Discuss with the children which cave would be the most exciting to set your scene in. If it is by the sea or a lake the knight may be able to get to it or escape from it by boat. If it is in the magical lake he may be able to call to the Lady of the Lake for help or it might pose extra dangers for him.

Once the decision is made and you have decided that the cave is to be set in a forest by a lake you need to start building the place. A good way to begin the process of setting the place is to go around the circle of children and sound-scape the cave so that you get a feeling of what it would sound like to be there. You want the children to experience the place in as many ways as possible. Ask the children to close their eyes and build the sound picture. Once this is done, ask the children to word-scape the cave using the feelings they got through listening. You could also play a piece of music to accompany the word-scape. If the place is beautiful and magical you could play the "Aquarium" movement from Saint-Saens' *Carnival of the Animals*. If it is threatening you could play a section from *Night on Bare Mountain* by Mussorgsky.

You can still use the flip chart or whiteboard and draw the cave and write ideas around it. Ask the questions – What does it look, sound, feel and smell like? Has it magical properties and if so, what are they? You may want to draw up a plan of what the place is like so that the children can visualise the setting. A lake surrounded by tall trees, with a mountain on one side in which is cut a treacherous path that leads to a ledge hiding a deep cave which is reached through a labyrinth of tunnels.

Place needs to have potential for writing; it needs to be drawn well so that the children can use the vocabulary they build as a resource for descriptive writing. You must get the children to think about dramatic tension and what the place offers to facilitate this tension. What would you feel like if you were standing in it?

Stage 4 Situation building

You now have your characters of the knight on the quest for a crystal that has been taken by the dragon. The creation of the situation can be either teacher or pupil led. How you facilitate the structure of the situation will be led by your initial catalyst and the characters you have created. Whether you are leading or facilitating, it is important that the situation should contain a conflict. This will help the later construction of the scene – it helps to have a tension between the characters. If they have different needs (i.e. the dragon needs the crystal to give to its master or to keep itself alive, and the knight needs the crystal because it heals the sick or can protect people), there is a conflict of interests to investigate in the situation.

It is always desirable to have a fail-safe situation to fall back upon; you may never need it but it will give you confidence to know it is there.

In our example we have the hero knight who needs the crystal. Why?

1. It has magical healing powers and the king is ill.
2. It belongs to a wizard and gives him powers to protect the kingdom, which is under attack and is falling.
3. It is the key to a magical land that the knight needs to get to on his quest.
4. It was once a queen who was turned into a crystal and the knight must take it to a good wizard to break the spell.

Why does the dragon need the crystal?

1. The dragon stole it because the crystal gives it great magical powers.
2. It gives the dragon its fire-breathing powers.
3. It is the dragon's heart and keeps it alive.
4. The dragon has stolen it to lure people to its lair so that it can kill and eat them.

When you are using positional drama for creative writing you may want to let the children offer possible situations and discuss their differing potential regarding their scope for strong story-telling. This will build the children's understanding of how conflict, time and place are crucial to creative writing. You decide, with the class, to take offer number 2 option, namely: *It belongs to a wizard and gives him powers to protect the kingdom, which is under attack and is falling.* You have chosen this option because it gives the situation great dramatic urgency. You ask the children what they would like to put into the situation and they come up with the following:

1. The dragon is evil and a liar.
2. The dragon will talk to the knight.
3. The knight has a dragon charm that makes the dragon unable to breathe fire when the dragon tries to kill him.

4. The dragon gives the knight a riddle or a problem to solve and if the knight solves or guesses the solution to the problem he can have the crystal.

5. The knight does get the crystal and the dragon is angry but goes back into the cave.

Stage 5 Entering the situation

Once the situation is agreed upon the central character is placed into it. One of the other characters is placed with the central character and they improvise around the situation, using their character outlines. You may want to give them a starting point with a line or an action. The line might be, "I know you are in the cave, dragon! Come out and face me!" or it may be that the knight must knock three times on the floor to summon the dragon. Initially the improvisation can be short with feedback to build the work, but the characters must include all the information that has been written on the board into the scene. You should check this as the scene builds. You will also want character work to go into the scene. If the dragon is evil this must be shown through dialogue, attitude and actions. You can change the children who are working on the scene around so that more than two children are involved.

1. The scene is discussed by the group as it is developed.

2. Children playing the characters must stay with those characters' point of view.

3. Children playing the characters describe what motivates their actions.

4. Character actions and feelings can be "thought-tracked" by children not involved in the scene and then agreed upon as right for that character.

5. The scene is scripted on the whiteboard (you may want to make a video of it for feedback).

Stage 6 Conclusion/reflection

If you are using positional drama to create characters and scenarios for creative writing you will be reflecting on the character/s and possible story ideas.

1. Was the character well drawn?

2. Did you believe in him or her?

3. Why did the characters function the way they did in the situation?

4. Was this believable?

5. What did the characters feel in different parts of the action?

You can discuss all the characters and their motivations and points of view and then move on to the strengths of your situation to build the children's understanding of the importance of place and dynamic tension.

- Was the place you created for the action strong?
- What made it effective?
- Was the situation strong?
- What worked well?

Then move on to written work, using the material you have worked on.

Options

1. Watch the scene.
2. Split the class into groups so that they can all work on the scene you have created.
3. Show the different ways in which the children have developed the work.
4. Discuss the fact that even with a structure there are different choices to make.

Follow-on work

1. Another character can be placed into the scene as required to further the story.
2. You may want to create another scene.
3. You can write up the scene, describing its physicality and tension.

Positional drama: studying literature

The stages of the different models stay the same, although the emphasis on the stages change, depending on what you are wishing to draw from the learning. When you are exploring a book you may want to analyse the writer's approach; the types of characters they create and the reasons why the story is set in a certain place and how the situations and tensions are created. This model uses *Oliver Twist*, which would be excellent for cross-curricular work tied in with history regarding study of the Victorian period.

Here is the model using *Oliver Twist*. You can adapt the model approach and techniques for any work you are studying. It may also be simplified and used for younger children's work. The stages remain the same.

Stage 1 Engaging catalyst

When you are studying a book your engagement catalyst will be dependent on what aspect of the book you want to work on. For example, if you are reading *Oliver Twist* you may begin the session by placing Oliver's mother's locket and ring (the key to unravelling the mystery of who Oliver is) in the centre of the circle. This will bring the story into the classroom in a tangible way, as a thriller that reading the book will solve. Questions might be "Who does this locket belong to?" Or "What do we know about this locket and ring?" Other catalysts might be:

1. Fagin's box of stolen goods.
2. A pocket watch.
3. Nancy's shawl.
4. An empty wooden bowl.
5. An engraving from the book.
6. Victorian money.
7. A clay pipe.
8. A picture of Bullseye or a dog lead.

FIGURE 5.7 Oliver Twist asking for more

Stage 2 Central and secondary characters

Central character

If you use the locket or the bowl to lead the children into creating Oliver you can then draw an outline of Oliver on the whiteboard and begin to collect all the information you have about him from the book. If you want to recap the chapters you are reading you can use the same model – draw Oliver and write up the information "what we know about this character so far". Then you can discuss how Dickens introduces the character and draws the reader into the story. You will also be looking at the Victorian era, so you will want to talk about this in regard to the social status of the characters. Do you see Oliver in the context of being in the workhouse or as one of the pickpockets, or of his standing at the end of the book? If the children create the poverty-stricken Oliver and Oliver with Mr Brownlow at the end of the story you would be looking at the Victorian social structure where children would starve or thrive, being dependent upon the wealth of the family into which they were born.

It is possible to conduct this "two faces of Oliver" role as a stand-alone exploration and write and reflect on what Dickens is telling us, as his readers, about the position of children in Victorian society. Dickens was a political novelist as his description of the baby Oliver denotes: "A parish child – the orphan of a workhouse, the humble, half-starved drudge, to be cuffed and buffeted through the world despised by all, and pitied by none."

If you are going to explore the scene between Nancy, Brownlow and Rose when Noah spies on them on London Bridge you will need to do a role on one of them. If you use a shawl as your catalyst you can build up the complex character of Nancy who is born into the Victorian poor working class but keeps her sense of right and wrong, and eventually dies for it.

Secondary characters

Your choice of secondary characters will be dependent upon the situations in the book you want to study. You might take Oliver as your character and when the children are familiar with the positional drama model you could give each table or "team" a character from the novel that they work on for ten minutes and then present to the group. You might put a clue on each table – a shawl for Nancy, an accounting sheet adding up stolen items for Fagin, a clay pipe for Bill Sykes – and ask the children to guess which character each item belongs to. When each group has completed their own raft of information about their character they can present to the class. You and the class can add any attributes that they may have forgotten. You can work on many characters because you are not devising, which takes more time and creative effort. You could let the children begin this process by remembering characters and then let them have reference to the book so that they can check their characters' information and details. They are studying how the writer has drawn and developed different characters in the story and the breadth of people, from Oliver, to Fagin, to Mr Bumble, to the sweet, wealthy Rose and the admirable, life-impoverished Nancy.

Emotional intelligence work around these characters would be in discussing how different people react to their various situations. Oliver is a great role model to investigate because he is a child, alone, facing insurmountable odds and surviving. He does not cry very often because he cannot allow himself that luxury – he keeps living despite what happens to him. How does he do this? What gives him the strength?

Nancy's decision to help Oliver escape, goes against our expectations. Why should she risk everything to help a child? Why not leave him to the fates like everyone else? Why does she feel guilty about kidnapping him? The children will relate to these people and the issues they face because, in their lives, they have choices to make and may well face uncomfortable situations which they have to survive and deal with.

Stage 3 Place

This will again be dependent upon what scene or scenes you want to study, but overall you will be looking at Victorian London and the social conditions of that time. As a background you may be studying the Poor Law, the workhouse, baby farms, children's employment, working conditions or class structure. You may be looking at the chapter in the workhouse when Oliver draws the short straw and must ask for more food, so the *place* becomes the workhouse. If you use the chapter where Nancy meets Mr Brownlow and Rose by London Bridge[3] with Noah spying on them your *place* will be London at night. You will want to create the feeling of the night and impending doom by reading the beginning of the chapter and researching what London was like at that time with the Bow Street Runners[4] and the dangers of ill-lit streets on this dark night.

The children can give you the following information from the text which you then write on the whiteboard.

- The church bell chimes the quarter hour –11.45 at night.
- Nancy is followed by Noah, unseen, along London Bridge.
- A very dark night.
- Black water not reflecting anything.
- Mist over the river Thames.
- St Paul's chimes midnight ("the death of another day").
- Brownlow and Rose arrive by hackney-carriage two minutes after midnight.
- They talk at the bottom of the second stage of three flights of steps on the Surrey (south side) of the bridge. Noah is listening beneath them.

Point out the many details Dickens uses when creating place to build time and tension as the characters gather together. Regarding writing techniques you can point out the way he used personification, such as the storehouses "frowning" sternly on the water and the churches being the "giant warders" of the bridge. Talk about the *place* being a bridge that is crossed from the affluent north of the river to the poorer and rougher south of the river (in Victorian times) and the characters descending the stairs into the depths and darkness. The place Nancy leads them to is a living hell.

Investigate why place is so crucial to a story.

- Why does Dickens set it on a bridge?
- Why does Dickens gain by setting it at midnight?
- How is time used to build tension (midnight, death of day, people arriving to the minute, everything coming to a head)?
- What would you lose if this chapter/scene was set in the daytime (e.g. in a park): the threat of a very dark London night, the ability for Noah to hide, fear of the dark and the unknown, the tension of whispering and not being able to see things clearly?
- Can you think of another strong place to set this scene?

Stage 4 Situation

The meeting of Nancy and Mr Brownlow and Rose is a great situation regarding points of view, as it provides strong tensions between the characters' needs and their enormously differing social perspectives. Brownlow hopes that Nancy can tell him something about Oliver but is not sure what it will be. He says he has come to "humour" her. Nancy is offered a chance to literally cross the bridge to a better life but won't leave the life she knows and the people who have stood by her, even though she is having visions of impending doom. Mr Brownlow is a good man, full of compassion in spite of his wealth and position, and is desperate to find Oliver.

Rose represents the flourishing young women who has had the good fortune of being wealthy in that society compared to Nancy, yet Nancy is a good women who is utterly crushed by her situation. Rose is also a good women, and Nancy is impressed and surprised by Rose's kindness to her.

Noah is spying on Nancy and will take the information back to Fagin – an act which we know will lead to her being killed by Sikes. All the characters have strong viewpoints and opinions of each other. You can either outline the scene from the chapter for the children to build on or convert the chapter into a script, as the dialogue is fulsome and powerful.

Stage 5 Entering the situation

Set up the tight area on the steps under the bridge and a place where Noah can hide to listen. This could be a table or a chair or part of the classroom. It is good to change around the children playing the characters so that more children can experience the scene. Set the convention that you may stop the action and ask other children to go into the scene and continue. This also keeps the children focused and involved, ready to enter the situation they have created.

The watching children will also feed into the process. Do as much of the scene as you wish. You may have scripted some of it or framed it as an improvisation, so that the children will know their characters' needs and make up their own version of the scene.

You can either work on specific sections or on one section in great depth, whatever gives you the learning outcomes you want. Remember: you can work initially with the whole class feeding into the scene and then form separate groups of four characters to work their scenes and then to come back and show their work to the class for feedback.

If using a script taken from the text:

1. Let the children run part or all of the scene; then ask the children what their characters are feeling. For example,
   - Nancy: Afraid, worried for Oliver and herself, not sure if she can trust Brownlow, admiring of Rose's kindness, lost, torn, scared by the offer of a new life. Feeling that something bad is going to happen because of her "visions".
   - Rose: Appalled by Nancy's life, scared of the dark, excited by the adventure, wants to help Nancy, becoming more aware of other people's lives and experiences.
   - Mr Brownlow: Initially suspicious about the safety of the place, concerned for Nancy, worried for Rose's safety, desperate to find Oliver, angry about Fagin and Monks.
   - Noah: Afraid about being discovered, angry at Nancy, excited that he can report back all this news to Fagin. [He does not speak but he is the threat of death hiding in the lower depths of the bridge.] Afraid of being discovered, shocked by what he hears, Nancy is betraying her own kind, angry, surprised.
   - Why does Dickens set it on the bridge?
2. Position some children behind each character and ask them to speak the character's needs and wishes at the end of their lines. Their thoughts might be:
   - Nancy: I must get away, I mustn't get caught, what I am doing is wrong. Why is she [Rose] being kind to me? Is anyone watching?
   - Brownlow: I must find Oliver, I'm afraid of this place, I mustn't put Rose in danger, I mustn't frighten this woman away, this woman is good, I want to help this woman, will I ever find Oliver?
   - Rose: Poor Nancy, the woman is so frightened, how poor she looks, how tired and old she looks, what will happen to her? I'm afraid for her, I want her to come away with us, do people really have lives as awful as this?

As the teacher, you are using the situation to investigate the characters' motives and inner worlds. They might say one thing but think another – such as Nancy saying "no" to the new life Mr Brownlow offers her but secretly wishing she could take it.

This exercise helps the children to understand how a writer builds a character's inner life through their actions. This is especially true for Nancy with whom we have a strong empathy because, like us, she cares about what will happen to Oliver. In her dangerous world, she is able to cling on to what is right. We admire her bravery and are appalled that she dies for it. Children have a great sense of what is fair; Dickens was a master at manipulating us to empathise with his characters as they encounter the often brutal randomness of fate and the social world they have been born into. What happens to Nancy isn't fair, as life often isn't fair to good people. This is a powerful and brilliantly structured scene to work on.

Use the book text to feed in character and place information, which is drawn so tangibly in the writing: we feel we are there, and the physicality of the characters. Nancy shudders, cries, looks distracted, and is violently agitated.

Stage 6 Conclusion/reflections

When working with a written text you are seeking to help the children to understand characters, story, structure and the way the writer crafts his work. You can discuss all the characters and their motivations and points of view:

1. Were the characters well drawn?
2. Why did you believe in them?
3. Why did they function in the way they did in the situation?
4. Was this believable?
5. How did their positions change in different parts of the action?
6. Why is the place and time so effective?

Then move into discussing the writer's power in creating this world for us:

■ How does the writer create place so strongly – pick out the language he uses.
■ How does he create fear in the reader?
■ Write a short part of the scene as a script and add stage directions to show how the characters speak and move.

You can move on to written work about the characters, perhaps exploring what Nancy and Rose's early lives may have been like.

■ What might have happened to Nancy if she had crossed the bridge with Rose and Mr Brownlow?
■ Why did Dickens write the ending for Nancy that he does in the book?

Positional drama: issue based

For issue-based work you should have a specific situation in which to place your characters that will focus on and support the issues you want to explore. You will need to offer this in a way that will engage the children and give them ownership of the process, to allow them to invest their own feelings and thoughts into the characters. You will also need to think about safety and holding the children in a structured framework so that they can investigate issues without feeling threatened. If bullying is an issue within the classroom you will need to consider how to use this model and whether it is appropriate to your circumstances. You may need to be careful when deciding what child takes the characters into the situation you create. The process of building characters and discussing situation should be given time. The process of preparing the work and the discussions you have during this process will be as meaningful as the situation you create. The process will need more than one session.

This model may be used for any issue you want to investigate in an open, thorough and safe way. You may want to look at bullying, racism, stealing, fighting or sharing. You are creating a group scene catalyst to enter and use to discuss issues, reasons for them happening and the options of different actions you can take. The template will work with all age groups and may be simplified to make it appropriate for younger children. The stages remain the same.

Issue-based model: bullying

As with all positional drama work we need to be very aware of keeping the children safe, especially if there are or have been bullying problems within the school or class. The positional drama work allows us to look at the issues through the characters we create. The teacher must be aware of children who may want to manipulate the situation or who may be worried and vulnerable regarding the situation. I have worked with this model using puppets, so that when we have created the characters using role-on-the-wall they go back to their team table and make a puppet of their character. It can be made simply out of newspaper folded and sticky-taped, or a drawn flat figure, or a more intricate version where you use the time to continue to engage the children in the character or the issue.

The making activity can release children to talk with you more freely. When working with a Year 6 group I brought in items of clothing so that the children could hold up different coloured tops to become the bully or the bullied child, or a cardigan became a teacher and a scarf became a mother. The act of holding up the clothes in front of them as they worked out the action of the situation they had set up became a shield for the children – a visual mask or disguise that helped them feel safe to take on the thoughts and actions of the characters.

Introducing the issue

We want to understand the bully and his or her social background. We create them and build their world. We might build a parent, a teacher, or other children who are important to the situation, and the person who is being bullied. We want to understand why they feel unable to stand up to the bully so we will give equal attention to their character and possibly build people from their world. If we enter issue-based work we must give it *time*. In the other positional drama models you may work faster, or, once the children understand the process, use parts of it when working creatively or with historical subjects. When you are investigating issues that are important to the children and which affect their lives you need to plan well and give time to investigate the emotions, situation, action and outcomes to make the process effective for understanding and change. We build the people we need and then we look at the situation from each individual's point of view. The teacher usually suggests the specific situation but can build the situation with the children if preferred.

- We can look at the relationship between the parent and the bully.
- We can look at the relationship between the bully and the person they victimise.
- We can look at the bully and why they act in the way they do.
- We can look at the feelings of the child who is victimised and what options they have.
- We can stay with each person and explore their issues, their feelings and their actions.

Stage 1 Engaging catalyst

The children sit in a circle. You place a battered pair of trainers in the middle of the circle (the more unisex the better). You say they belong to someone and you are all going to build the character together.

If you want to lead the work more at this point you could introduce the shoes by saying, "These belong to a boy/girl who is about your age. They aren't very happy or popular at school – although children pretend to like them because they are a bit afraid of what they might say or do. Let's build up a picture of what he/she is like." Discuss the shoes: you are detectives. What are you able to discern from them? Do they belong to a boy or a girl? Does that boy or girl come from a wealthy or a poor family?

Stage 2 Central and secondary characters

Central character

You can now take the learning to the whiteboard and build your character. You can write down and draw upon this information for written work that will follow.

You now begin to ask specific questions to feed into the situation you want to create. Draw a shape of a person on your whiteboard — you or your TA or a designated child can write down what is said about the person on the board. You may draw in brief descriptions of other people around the character, such as mum, dad, a friend or a teacher. Using the shoes as evidence, you have decided that the central character is a boy:

- What does he look like (eyes, hair, size, weight, height, does he bite his nails)?
- Where does he live?
- Who does he live with?
- Which people are important to him?
- What does he like doing?
- What does he care about?
- Who are his friends?

You must keep these features realistic: challenge the children if they go into the realms of fantasy or contradict each other – they are working with the character they are creating. They must build on what is offered and not break it down.

Remember that once the children offer you a fact, such as "He doesn't like school" you should ask "Why?" in order to build on their understanding of the character. There are reasons why people don't like things, or why they are angry, and you want to encourage the children to analyse and understand behaviour through this exercise. When they create their bully they need to create a background and a set of circumstances for him.

Dan – created by a class of Year 4s.

- Poor family background
- Looks hard
- Doesn't take care of himself
- His jeans are dirty
- No washing machine
- Old trainers, can't afford new ones
- Likes football but is no good at it
- Likes writing stories
- Wants to be cool
- In trouble for stealing at school
- Wanted new trainers
- Mum involved with new man, Steve
- Dan gets in the way
- Dan doesn't see his dad

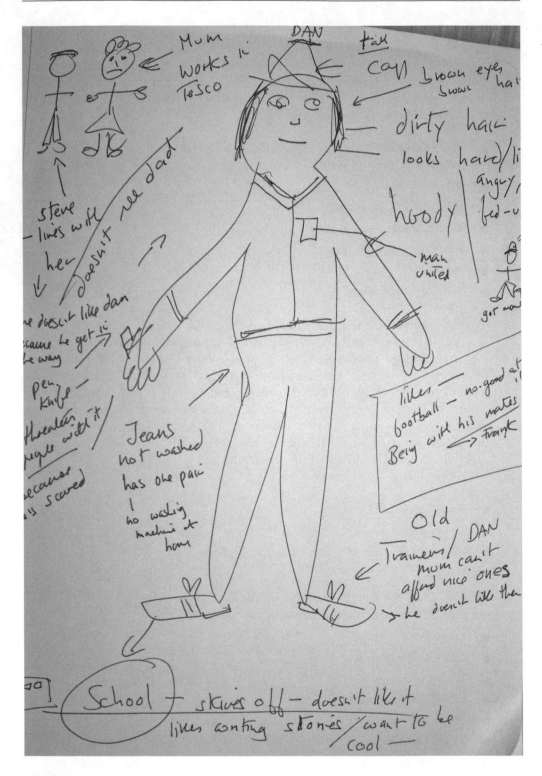

FIGURE 5.8 Dan, created by Year 4s

- Fed up
- Angry
- Doesn't like school and skives off
- Friend called Frank – has money
- Keeps a knife to frighten people because he's scared.

(NB: this information was written up again in more legible handwriting. When the children's offers come quickly the quality of the handwriting can suffer!)

It is interesting to see the amount of information here that can be used to build the character in a three-dimensional way. Dan likes football but he fails at it – if he was good at football and it helped him to make friends or feel good about himself, how might this change his personality? The character information gives you a chance to question how the boy feels and why he might be angry. The children also offered that he likes writing stories but he wants to be seen to be "cool". This is also interesting because it allows us to talk about why liking a certain aspect of learning would not be seen as being "cool" by Dan. Why not? The children make you offers from their own experience and understanding; when you discuss these points with them through the medium of an imaginary person they are creating, this gives you the chance to talk directly to their issues, perceptions and fears.

The children have created a character that is very human and believable. He "gets in the way" at home because his mother has a new boyfriend. When I asked the children how Dan might feel, they replied, "fed up" and "angry". They were drawing a picture of a child from a dysfunctional home who found it difficult to be with adults and children when in school. When I asked why he carried a knife to frighten people one of the boys said it was because Dan "was scared". They were keen to give reasons for the way Dan looked, and that he wanted to be able to dress better and be like other kids who "had stuff". There was an understanding of Dan in the group but the children were clear that they were creating a child who would bully, and that they would not like him.

Secondary characters

In issue-based work you will need to keep secondary characters to a minimum; you want to keep the characters real and it can become difficult to work with too many, since you may want to do a role-on-the-wall with all of the characters. You need to be clear who you will want to use in the situation so you will want to plan ahead. In this scenario I wanted to create a home life for Dan so he that would be seen in a wider context. We need to understand what makes him bully in school. I wanted a parent or carer figure, male or female, and this was up to the children. They created a mother who was tired all the time and wanted to be with Steve and not Dan. (This idea came from the children: you will get different offers when creating this character. You can add to them and build in more reasons for the mother to be unsupportive of Dan; she may be stressed about money or think he doesn't like her.) The process of building characters allows you to explore issues of relationships and parenting with the children in the safe framework of imagined people. The bully could be a boy or a girl: remember you can leave this open for the children to decide or lead it with your initial catalyst obviously belonging to a boy or girl.

There will be other characters that you want to build into your situation and they are created in the same way. You can take them from the people identified as being important to the character in the first stage and people you want to put into the situation. In this scenario we created a mother who worked but didn't earn a lot of money. She didn't live with Dan's father but with another man called Steve. Dan didn't get on with his mother whom he felt "didn't want him around". You will need to be aware that children may sometimes offer part of their own story to you or, often, part of a television "soap opera" story. If they are using their own stories you will need to filter and join ideas together so that one child is not exposed. This is easy to do as you will have a choice of options from the children. If they offer television scenarios challenge them to question the characters and make sure the scenario fits in with the people you are creating. Say, "This is our story. We don't need to copy stories from television, we can make our own stories that mean something to us."

In this scenario we also created Dan's friend Ken and the child who was being bullied – George — and a teacher. George was clever but didn't have friends, so Dan targeted him because he was jealous and knew that George was often on his own. George was scared of Dan, who threatened to "get him" outside of school if he told anyone about the bullying. He forced George to give him his sweets, called him names and pushed him over in the playground when they were alone. Ken was in Dan's class and was both impressed and scared of him. The teacher, who "got up at six every morning to prepare for work", taught in Dan's class. We did a role-on-the-wall for all of these characters. You may not use the mother in the initial situation but she is important in understanding Dan, just as George's family background is important in understanding why he gets bullied and why he cannot ask for help in his situation.

Stage 3 Place

The place was a quiet area of the school playground. This gave the children an opportunity to talk about the playground environment. Was it a safe and happy place? Did everyone have the same experience of the playground? If not, why not?

We talked about safe areas of the playground as well as areas that sometimes could not be seen by the staff on duty as they patrolled. Some children talked about not liking certain games that were played or wanting to have formal activities during playtime. I allowed the discussion to continue and then asked if we wanted to create a playground that wasn't the children's own school playground. The offer was made that this playground would have an area where the children were not allowed to go near some bins and that George went there to hide from Dan, who found him. We agreed upon this and moved on to Stage 4 (Situation), as this was already beginning to be opened up by one of the children's idea of George being found by Dan.

Stage 4 The situation

You can either let the children build the situation or present them with a fait accompli.

In this model I adopted the idea of George hiding from Dan but asked the children why he was hiding. Offers were:

- Dan always gets him at playtime. (Why?) Because it makes him feel good to frighten someone/it's a habit/George makes him angry/George makes him jealous. (Why?)
- George has come top in a test and Dan has said he will get him if he does.
- George is afraid of Dan and always hides at playtime – but he doesn't tell anyone.
- George has got new trainers and Dan is jealous.

We agree on the following situation and give it a brief. The brief can be either a loose framework or very detailed. The following scenario was worked on by the children in some detail, as I wanted to talk about bullying issues of fear and denial in the process of building the scene:

1. Dan and Ken find George behind the bins.
2. Dan is going to tell George to put his new trainers into the school bin, "or else":
   - Dan will do it
   - George is scared but won't take his shoes off
   - Ken tries to persuade Dan to come away and play football (he is worried).
3. An older girl sees them and tells them to stop:
   - They say that aren't doing anything
   - George doesn't say anything to her and doesn't leave. (Why?)
4. Dan tells the girl to leave them alone and she goes away:
   - The girl asks George to go with her – he doesn't
   - Dan and Ken say they are friends with George
   - Girl leaves and Dan resumes bullying.
5. The bullying gets worse:
   - Ken tells Dan they should leave in case the girl comes back
   - Dan tells Ken to stay and get George's shoes unless he gives them money
   - George says he hasn't got any money
   - Dan says he has to steal some – they talk.

6. The girl brings back a teacher who sees the boys:

- The teacher asks what is going on
- Dan, Ken and George all say "Nothing".

Stage 5 Entering the situation

We set up an area for the bin and where the rest of the playground is to be located. All the children become the audience and are allowed to raise their hands and offer ideas or lines for the scene as it builds. We have agreed that we will not allow our actors to get physical but if they feel that the character would do so they are allowed to voice their actions. For example, "If you don't put your trainer in the bin *I* will! – *I go over and Ken holds George's arms and I take off his shoe and throw it in the bin.*" We will then safely act out the action. This allows the children time to see how huge the action is and how we look after each other as we act it out. It becomes a contrast to the potential violence of the action and places it in a clear context. You should change over the children who are portraying the characters so that others get a chance to enter the situation. When they do so they must build on the point of view that has been made by the group.

Points of view

The action is played out with sections of the children becoming the thoughts of Dan, Ken and George. As they speak we may repeat a line and then ask the children playing them to express their characters' feelings. We are working from each character's point of view and have to remain true to their emotions in the situation. This also occurs with the girl who intervenes. We need to know why she is strong enough to do this and how she feels. Is Ken afraid of what is happening or is he empowered by it? Why doesn't George shout out, fight or run away? What does the teacher think when she sees what is going on? What does she do?

Stage 6 Reflection

A great deal of thinking would have occurred within the process of this work. You have been investigating the issue of bullying through building the characters, their home lives and school lives, and reasons for action or non-action. You have been exploring feelings about playtime and the safety of the school environment. You need to bring these issues together in reflecting on what you have learnt. You must spend time with each character and try to understand their point of view and motivation.

There are lots of points to reflect on. Whose fault is it that Dan is a bully? Is it anyone's fault? What could change him? How could the playtimes have been made safer? What should George have done to help himself and why couldn't or didn't he do these things? What does Ken think in the situation? Why does

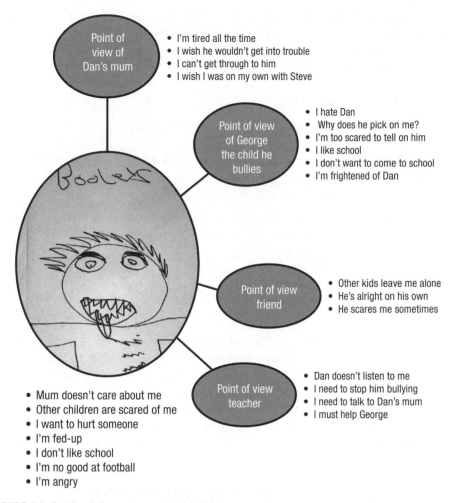

FIGURE 5.9 Positional drama: issue-based bullying

he try to stop it? Is he afraid of Dan or is he a good friend? How can George stop it happening again? If he cannot prevent it how can he get help?

You may want to talk about how things could have been different for the characters. What could they or someone else have done to help them in their situation?

Further work

You may want to create a scenario for Dan and his mother or Dan and the teacher or the teacher talking with Dan and George. A good title for more positional drama work or written would be: What happened next? You can use the characters' various points of view to tell the story from different angles. Children may want to look at the school's bullying policy and talk about what would have been effective for Dan and George.

In issue-based work there may be elements you will want or need to follow up, especially if bullying is an issue for your class. You have opened up a pathway for discussion and the possibility of changing the way people will react to or help the vulnerable children in their class.

Other issue-based work

This model may be used for any issue-based subject:

- Remember that you can guide the work and set it in your own context.
- When exploring religious or racist issues you could suggest specific topics such as, beliefs, or ethnic origins.
- You can set the frameworks of character, place and situation while giving the children ownership by using role-on-the-wall.
- When you set up the situation you can use simple puppets, half masks or representation objects to denote character. There are many ways to distance the children from the characters they have created if you feel it is appropriate to do so.

You are creating the people and their worlds together through your and the children's experiences and understanding of them. The initial phase of creating the characters that people your situation can be extended so that the children are able to research backgrounds and religions.

It is safe to use this technique when working on issues such as racism because you can project the children's understanding and experience through the characters they are creating. No child should ever be allowed to feel exposed when using positional drama.

The Story Web: a visual aid for understanding story structure and creative writing

This technique is an excellent visual aid that allows you to build stories or narratives with the children in a visual and kinaesthetic way. Children often have problems in shaping stories: they are able to create short pieces in a specific situation but find it difficult to progress their stories into a wider structure. This technique illustrates the journeys a story can go on and the frameworks you can place them in. It shows:

- How stories/narratives are built
- A visual aid to the progress and shape of a story
- The building of a narrative with each page being a new chapter of the story
- The options the writer has – how one event can move on into others
- A way to frame stories before the children write them so that they know what they are going to include into each chapter or paragraph.

FIGURE 5.10 Teacher leads the Story Web with a class of Years 5 and 6

You can explain all of the above to the children when you are working with the story web, as the visual aid of the paths of different stories they have built is set out on the floor in front of them.

Technique

Place a piece of paper with a character's name on it in the centre of the floor.

You may have built this character through a catalyst and a role-on-the-wall exercise so you will have an idea of age, social context, time period, place and friends – or you can say, "This is a boy aged 14 called Ben." Write down the name on the paper and something that has just happened to the character that allows the children to make a decision and following action (e.g. Ben is at home when an important letter arrives addressed to him).

Split your class into groups of six and ask them to decide on a series of events that follow on from each other from the initial catalyst.

In the following scenario we have used an important letter as the catalyst for four different stories. The letter can contain anything the children want (e.g. an object, a map, a book, a mysterious invitation, a secret code, a legacy or an offer of a football trial with a famous club). Each group decides what the letter contains and builds up a story chapter by chapter. The children write down the information

112

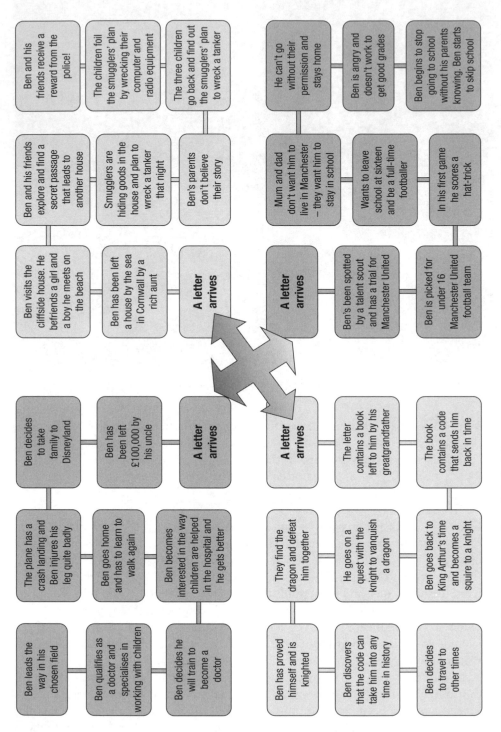

FIGURE 5.11 Different ideas created by the arrival of a letter

contained in each chapter on a piece of paper and connect the pieces with string or masking tape so that they can begin to build a web radiating out from the initial catalyst. Each group builds up from the catalyst using one piece of paper. You can brief each group to go for a certain type of story (e.g. magical, historical, adventure, fairy-tale). By the end of the exercise your floor will be covered with imaginative story ideas that all come from the initial idea or "first chapter", which is the arrival of the letter.

Extensions

1. Writing the chapters up in groups of two to the briefs you have worked out and putting them together as a team book.

2. Building a story for characters you have created from role-on-the-wall before writing it down.

3. Using the Story Web to break down the chapters in a book you are studying.

4. Using the same technique in PSHE when discussing religions or citizenship (e.g. place a "baby" on the floor and create the Story Web of all the services and people he will meet during his life as a citizen).

6

Exploring Games: Learning in Motion

Social interaction and building imagination

When we improvise (make up things) in a group we are using ourselves and our experience, making us exposed and vulnerable. Remember that children, like teachers, may be scared of the idea of "drama" and making up things on the spot. I know teachers can be very wary of anything that sounds as if it may include "acting" from the many times working with teachers when I say, "And now for some role play!" and everyone turns pale. Then I say, "Remember this feeling of fear at the thought that I might put you on the spot in front of each other, because that's how some children will feel in your classroom when faced with something new: disempowered and a little scared. You, of course, being grown-ups, can handle the fear better." We then go on to have a great time together by acknowledging that something can be scary and then saying how we will make it safe. This puts everyone at ease and allows them to enter into the work feeling relaxed and more willing to try it. This is as true for children with their powerful adults in the classroom as it is for us in situations when we are being taught or trained by others.

The children may think that "doing some drama" entails putting on a play or acting, or being watched by the entire class while they "can't do something". You must ensure that they, and you, don't work under pressure. I prefer to call these exercises "exploring games" where we wake up our imagination. You are using the children's instinctive ability to play to enable their learning. In truth you are working at a deep intrapersonal and interpersonal level with them, analysing behaviour, building resilience, building their imaginative capacity and problem solving, but this experiencing and learning is cloaked in the fun of working together.

Rules for exploring games

Safety: creating the environment for the work

1. Always explain that no one will be "put on the spot" unless they want to be.

2. You know the exercises but the children don't, so demonstrate them to start with and check that everyone understands what is required.

3. Set up a system whereby the children can "pass" in an exercise or repeat what someone else has done. Don't hover or focus too much on children who are shy at the start of experiential work. (Confidence to join in will grow, but this may take time for vulnerable children.)

4. Explain that when discussions are required in exercises everyone needs to listen to offers. Noise levels may get loud but they should remain group-conversational. Use this element of the work to teach the children to regulate their noise levels and to do it for each other.

5. Place vulnerable children near you and your TA in circle games.

High stakes and belief – creating the motivation

As the teacher, you are creating the context for the work that will take place. Your energy and the strength of your belief in the children will be what empowers them to push or challenge themselves in their imaginative and creative process. Can you remember learning to swim, ride a bike or jump a stream with a parent saying, "you can do it! Come on just have a try – I'm here. I believe/know you can do it!" and the feeling of accomplishment and pride in ourselves and joy in our parent's pleasure when we achieved it? This is the safe adult pushing the child out into the world to experience and experiment with their capabilities. This is why many adults say they were inspired by their teachers to enter the jobs they do. They become a teacher because the most rewarding time of their life was at primary school with an inspirational teacher, or they become writers because story time opened up their imaginations to creative writing. You should never underestimate the power of your belief in the children you teach for the children you teach.

1. Always give your experiential work a status of importance and exciting challenge. This is to engage the children in the process.

2. Set up a system so that the work will be challenging but you believe that they can succeed: "This is asking a lot of you, because you'll need to work together and think of lots of imaginative ideas, but I think /believe you/we can do it!"

   Don't always use the same language to introduce the exercises but you must challenge them to meet the task and express your belief that the children can achieve it.

3. Some exercises work well when the challenge to do something is timed. This can focus the thinking and motivate making choices. If you are working with one group that is slower than the others give them all the same time. You will usually find that children who have issues with reading and are consequently slower will not be when approaching work kinaesthetically. If you have children who have processing problems make sure that they understand the work required. Repeat it or work with them for a while at the start of the exercise so that they are not exposed but can check they know what is required.

The affirmation sandwich! – Supporting and growing confidence

The *affirmation sandwich* is the key to growing a child's confidence; it is an easy technique and it is good to make it a habit. The affirmations can be quite gentle, but the language you use empowers the child to try harder and develop. I have used it to great effect with both children and adults: we all respond to positive affirmation.

Affirm and add and affirm. Make it part of the way you encourage them to be brave in their work. Their confidence comes from your support and your belief in and opinion of them:

1. "Well done! That was very interesting/strong/brave/imaginative. Why don't we try adding xxxxxx to it? I think we can make it even better."

2. "I like the way you did x and x and x. Let's try again, adding y and z, and see what happens. Well done!"

3. This way you are always strengthening the children's confidence in what they have made and creating a pattern of adding or retrying and improving. It should become part of your teaching toolbox:

   - Affirm
   - Add
   - Affirm.

Analysing – drawing the learning from the experience

The exploring games give you the opportunity to get the children to look at themselves and the way they work together – their social skills are paramount in allowing most of these games to succeed. At the end of each game analyse what has happened. You are detectives searching out what worked and what did not.

- Did you enjoy that?
- What did you enjoy about it? (Point out that different people like different elements.)
- What was hard and what was easy?

- Why was it hard or easy?
- Did you understand what other people needed from you? How?
- Why wasn't everyone included? (If they weren't and if it's appropriate to discuss it.)
- How could we have solved that/done that better?
- What could we add to the game?

We have talked about play and its value function as a developmental tool. A child plays with objects to explore and discover them. We can instigate imaginative play in the classroom to explore ourselves, each other, other lives and experiences.

All the exercises may be used across all age ranges – you simply temper them to the level of the children with whom you are working. When models are specific to ages this is indicated, but the shapes of all of the exercises are for you to use imaginatively in the classroom or hall.

Remember to work initially in your comfort zones and to extend the work as the children grow in confidence. An exercise may be used in the last ten minutes of a lesson, start small and grow big! This work should be exciting, creative, enriching and fun. Remember: we laugh when we feel safe, when we feel confident and when we understand something together. Laughter is a great socialising tool for relaxing children and bonding groups.

All the exercises and models that follow are explained and set out for you to use. A child should always succeed to his or her full potential in them. They are not competitive but cooperative; no one fails.

Who are you?

This is a game that is easy and may be played as a start to the day. Many teachers play versions of it for circle time in Reception and Year 1, but it is also a good game for extending and using across the years. Keep vulnerable children close to you or to your TA to help them feel safe. Use *high stakes*. Say, "This is a tricky game that takes a lot of concentration/care but I think we can do it!"

Roll the name – basic method

1. Sit in a circle. Roll a ball across the circle to child A.
2. Child A receives the ball and says their own name and rolls it to child B.
3. Child B says their own name and rolls the ball across the circle to child C.
4. Child C says their own name and rolls the ball across the circle to child D, and so on.
   - Encourage the children to roll the ball gently and with focus.
   - Encourage eye contact: "Look at the person you are rolling it towards."
   - If certain children don't roll the ball to everyone challenge them to do this.
   - If appropriate, ask the children how it might feel to not receive the ball.

Extensions – building knowledge

1. The child says the name of the person they are rolling the ball to.

2. The child says their own name and then the name of the person they are rolling the ball to. (This is good for processing and sequencing thoughts: it's harder than you think.)

3. Building vocabulary. When you receive the ball you have to say: a colour/an animal/a bird/a country/a story character/something you'd find in a kitchen/a sport, and so on.

Revision exercise

1. The children roll the ball and have to say something about a subject or project they have studied (e.g. something about India/the Victorians/the Second World War).

What do you feel about [. . .] ?

A roll–the–ball "feelings game". Be sure the subject you pick is appropriate. Sometimes children run out of words quite quickly depending on the subject. Remind them that they must use "feelings" words.

■ The teacher picks a subject – such as school holidays.

■ The teacher says the subject and rolls the ball slowly across the circle.

■ The child receives the ball and expresses a feeling about the initial subject (i.e. happy/excited/expectant).

■ The ball is rolled to another person who as they receive it must express a feeling about the initial subject.

■ The teacher asks for the ball back and gives another subject (e.g. friends/school/television/spelling tests/football).

Extensions

■ Choose a subject such as "swimming" and ask the children to suggest words they associate with the action.

Cooperation and non-verbal communication

Eye contact line

Ask the children to get in a line going from the lightest coloured eyes to the darkest coloured eyes. Pitch the difficulty of this exercise at what you feel they are capable of. Take part: it gives you the chance for making eye contact with children who may be shy with you. Either you, your TA or a child checks the line to see if it is correct.

1. You may help them to organise the line-up.
2. The children may do it together without your help.
3. The children have to form a line with no talking – just through eye contact and actions.
    - This is good for shy children, who will look at each other in the excitement of the challenge.

Analysis – social working

- Is this an easy exercise to do silently?
- What strategies do you need to use to do it silently?
- If someone takes the lead in the exercise how do they do it?
- Is it hard to look someone in the eye? Why?

Extended work – understanding faces

Working in pairs, pretend you need to describe your partner's face to someone over the telephone. Give as much detail as possible. Make a drawing of the person and write down a description of their face; talk about their expression.

Sit in a circle. The teacher rolls a ball to someone who then has to describe another person in the circle without looking at them. The children have to guess who is being described.

Height line

Ask the children to form a line going from the tallest to the shortest person. Either you, your TA or a child checks the line to see if it is correct.

1. You can help them to do this.
2. They do it with each other.
3. They have to do it with no talking – just through eye contact and actions.

Analysis

- Is this an easy exercise to do silently?
- What strategies do you need to use to do it silently?
- If someone takes the lead in the exercise how do they do it?
- Does it make a difference if you are tall or short?

Point out that height differences will change over time. Help the children to feel positive about being short and discuss and, if appropriate, analyse the issues around being small.

Extending work

Question: What animals or insects are small but powerful? Answer: Poisonous snakes and small tree frogs. (One of the most deadly creatures on the planet is a mosquito that carries malaria.) Discuss the strength of ants.

The factory game 1

(Building affect) It's not what you do but the way that you do it!

Stand in front of the children and say you are going to "say" something to them without speaking. Using your hands, signal "Stand up" (hands out in front of you, palms up and raise them). Signal "Sit down" (reverse action). Ask the children how they understood what you wanted them to do. They will say, hopefully, by watching your actions. Explain how we communicate through actions.

1. Split the children into small groups, where vulnerable children will be supported to follow.
2. Give each group a phrase to get across to another group using actions.
3. The children must discuss how they are going to do this and then all perform the action together.
4. Each group will perform their action and the rest of the class will guess what they are trying to "say". We are building their level of understanding social signals.

You are in a very noisy factory where no one can hear anyone else speak. One group needs to signal to the other group one of the following. Write down or whisper them to the groups.

- Time for a drink.
- Come here.
- Be quiet.
- I'm hungry.
- I want to sleep.
- Go away.
- You're crazy.
- What time is it?
- This smells nice.
- I don't like you.
- I don't know.
- I don't care.

Analysis

- How do we use our facial expressions to let people know how we are feeling?
- How do we use our bodies to let people know how we are feeling?
- In what ways do teachers signal to us?
- What ways and when do we signal to each other?

Extended work

1. Work out a factory situation where three people have a "conversation" about what they are making without speaking. By watching we must know:

   - Who is the boss.
   - What they are making.
   - If they like what they are making.

2. Two people meet on a bench – they have a conversation without speaking.
   If it helps, give the brief. For instance, they have just seen a football game or they are watching a football game (perhaps supporting different sides so that there actions are opposite one another as one team scores). Alternatively, they have just come back from a shopping expedition. Has one managed to find great things and the other one hasn't? Is one rich and the other poor? We must know:

   - If they like each other.
   - What they have been doing (e.g. shopping).

   Analyse these actions after you have watched them. How much did you understand? How clear were the actions?

   Have twenty minutes where no one speaks but you all communicate with each other in action!

The factory game 2

It's not what you say but the way that you say it!

This is an amusing game of exploration that follows on from the previous exercise.

The factory games need to be delivered effectively in order to have a full impact upon the children, because tonal communication isn't as easy to explain as facial and physical communication.

Model tonal communication by explaining that as well as communicating with our faces and our physicality we communicate through the tone of our voice, such as saying to a baby, "No! Don't touch that heater, it's hot!" Ask the children how a baby, who may not understand language, would know that you wanted them not to do something. It's not what you say but the way that you say it:

- Tone − how loud or soft?
- Pitch − low or high? (We have a three-and-a-half-octave speaking range)
- Speed − slow and well enunciated.
- Fast − urgent.
- Happy − upbeat and light.
- Angry, harsh − biting off the ends of words.

Situate two children facing each other across a desk (e.g. a shopkeeper and a customer). The children can say only one word − and use this word to communicate what they want.

1. Someone is taking a jumper back to a shop because it is faulty.
2. They want a replacement
3. The shopkeeper looks at the jumper but refuses to replace it.
4. The only word the customer can say is "sausages".
5. The only word the shop keeper can say is "bacon".
6. They must say the words in such a way that we can understand what is happening.

Physical contact − the magic hand

This is useful regarding power and what it feels like to have control or to have to follow. It is a good exercise in trust, since the leader must ensure that the follower is safe. It is a good exercise in showing a magical link (e.g. A wizard and charmed person or Oberon and Puck). It is also a good exercise to use before moving into a piece of positional drama on power or bullying.

1. One child is A and one is B.
2. A lifts his hand and makes it flat. He can then move himself and his hand position.
3. B must keep his face close to A's hand, looking at it all the time.
4. A moves his hand and B follows it wherever it goes (up, down, around, etc.).
5. A must move B but keep B safe at all times.
6. Switch over so that B leads and A follows.

Extensions

- Add words: A says, "You must follow." B says, "I must obey."
- Add words: A says, "You must follow." B says, "I won't" but B still follows while trying to resist.
- Maintain a distance between A and B but A must still follow B's hand actions.

Analyse

- Ask the children which role they preferred and to analyse why.
- What does it feel like to lead someone (powerful, responsible, tiring)?
- Why would we want to lead? In what situations does there need to be a leader?
- What does it feel like to follow (easy, hard, frustrating, boring)?
- Why would we want to follow? In what situations is it good to follow?

Who am I? Name and action

This is an affirmation and socially bonding game where the children get to hear their name being said by everybody and everyone learns something about each other. It builds group feeling and self-esteem — in drama situations children can be nervous, especially if in a new group. This game gets everyone working together and is affirming for all. Children can pass, or the teacher, TA or other children can make offers for them.

- Stand in a circle.
- Each child says their name with an action mimicking something they really enjoy doing (e.g. a hobby).
- All the group repeats the child's name and the action together.
- The repetition must be as accurate as possible to encourage good observation.
- The level of sound the children make saying each child's names is empowering for children who may not be singled out often, or who do not operate well in social groups.
- If you have very shy or vulnerable children in the class make sure that they are with you or with your TA.
- Get the children to speak out but not to shout – they must do the action together. You are teaching them to become sensitive to each other as a group.

Extensions

- Reflect together on the different likes expressed and point out similarities between children.
- Ask about their hobbies — develop in literacy or shared conversational work.
- Change the games to actions of what the children *don't* like.
- Everyone has to mime a sport.
- Everyone has to express a feeling, perform the action of that feeling and everyone copies it.

Focusing and calming game

This game will instantly quieten a group and get them to work as a team. It is good for socialising a class as it will not work unless the children are cooperative and really concentrate on the signals of when someone is going to move.

Get all the children to stand in a circle, and place an object in the centre of the circle.

Explain that the exercise is not a race where someone has to get to the centre first but an exercise in cooperation, where everyone is trying to get to the object in the centre as a group. They must not talk or nod to one another to move. If they do create a pattern of movement through non-verbal communication, congratulate them on their strategy and get them to begin again. The challenge is for them to become acutely aware of each other and each person's intention to move.

- All the children must focus on the object and move towards it.
- They must move one at a time.
- If they move together they must go back to their original circle position.
- Play the game slowly so that the children focus and become aware of each other.
- Try to get the children to sense when someone is going to move.
- The children must all facilitate each other to arrive at the object together.

Extension – at desks or standing in circle

- Get the children to count from 1 to 20.
- They must speak one at a time.
- If two or more children speak together you will have to go back to the start of the count.

7

Emotional Learning in Class Delivery

Expressing emotions

When we talk about emotional intelligence we often ask children, "How are you feeling?" or we ask them to choose from a scale of faces (from happy to sad) to give an indication of how they are feeling. Feelings can be difficult to analyse and express, and adults can find it difficult to express their feelings and emotional responses.

During a teacher's Inset on emotional intelligence I did an exercise, often used with children, where a ball is rolled across a circle and the participants are asked to respond to a word, name or statement with the way they feel about that word or statement as the ball reaches them. For example, *Christmas* might get the responses happy, excited, stressed, jittery, frazzled, worried, overwrought. Other starter words used were *Holidays, Pay, Family* and *Relationships*; gradually becoming more personal and exposing. When we reached the more personal areas the teachers became hesitant and the words were sometimes hard to find:

- Because we don't discuss our emotions readily.
- Because it is hard to find the vocabulary to express emotions.
- Because we may not want to share our feelings in a group.

This is as true for children as it is for adults. It is important to accord the children we are working with the right to their privacy, and to respect them for sharing their feelings with us.

Emotions and feelings are often experienced as a state of being, or in reaction to something that happens. They are not initially reasoned. Being able to reason and analyse our feelings is necessary to regulate them. Thus, if we can facilitate children to find words for feelings to help understand and identify them, we may be able to help them regulate how they behave when they are facing difficult emotions. It is important to make the children aware that there is a language for emotions. You want the children to understand that feelings, which can be overwhelming and frightening, can be described, understood and contained by words.

The following exercises and games will help to facilitate the understanding of emotions. Some are specified for certain year groups, but all models may be simplified, developed and extended for use as you see as being appropriate for your classroom delivery.

Feelings cards (Reception – Year 2)

The purpose of this exercise is to look at emotions, what they are, and how they are expressed in a safe way. "Emotion" is not an easy word to understand, whereas "feeling" is often used and will be more familiar to the children. When working with younger children you can use the cards with the word and a drawing or an image of a face which expresses that emotion. You need to aid the child's understanding of the emotion/feeling that you are exploring.

Basic feeling words for younger children might be: *happy, angry, worried, sad*. Children often choose the word "sad" to describe difficult feelings, since it is one of the more accessible and frequently used words to describe complex feelings to a child. It is often used by young children to describe their feelings when talking to social workers. When a grandparent dies and adults try to help a child understand their feelings of loss they do not use words like distraught or bereft but words such as *sad* or *unhappy*. Children can and do experience great depths of emotional feeling and it is important that the adults around them give them language to help express these feelings. When foster carers and adopters are trained they are advised to help build the emotional vocabulary of the children they will care for to give them ways to begin to express the often frightening, confusing emotions of separation, loss and anger that they may experience.

Always start your work on feelings with positive emotions (*happy, surprised, amazed, love, cheerful, excited*) before moving on to the negative emotions (*sad, angry, disgusted, grumpy, annoyed, fearful*). You will cover many emotions as you read and work on stories, and in creative writing when you are building characters, and in history when you are studying real people. Use the feelings cards to explore in depth and as a quick aid to help the children empathise with people and situations, both fictional and factual.

Here is the model:

We want to explain and understand the feelings/emotional words we are considering, and we will approach them in a three-stage process as follows:

1. What the feeling (emotion) means
2. What the feeling (emotion) looks like
3. Describe the feeling using other words and demonstrate it.

Explaining the stages in detail for the word "Happy"

Choose a story to read to the children which contains a character who is clearly happy. You may keep the exercise to one happy character or look at more than one.

1. What the word means – using a character you have told a story about:
   - Show the children the card, read the word *Happy* to them and point out the face on the card.
   - Ask them what they think the word means, and help out as necessary.
   - Talk about the story you have just read and ask them what character/s in the story was/were happy in it.
   - Ask them why they think the character/s was/were happy.
2. What the feeling looks like.
   - Get the children to stand in a circle and think about the happy character. Ask them to pretend to be that happy character. You might choose a specific, happy moment in the story.
   - Get half the children to watch the other half being the happy character and ask them to describe how the children showed they were happy with their faces and bodies. You can help if necessary by describing the children's *happy* actions (i.e. they smile, they jump up and down, they giggle, they have bright eyes).
3. Describing the feeling using alternative words.
   - You can end the process by thinking of other words that are similar in meaning to happy, or how you would describe someone who was feeling happy using alternative words.
   - Get all the children to pretend to give each other a present that makes them really happy. They might tell you what the present could be. The children might say, "Here is a lovely present for you!" and the others can reply in a very happy way: "Thank you!"

The children will begin to understand the technique and know that you are giving them a fun and safe way to look at feelings. Once they have understood and played with the word *Happy* you could try giving them a feeling that is opposite, such as *Sad*.

Model example

Here is a model that will look at the feeling/emotion of sadness. You have a feelings card with the word *Sad* and a the picture of a sad face (if you think it will be helpful to the children).

An interesting story to work with would be *Lost and Found* (Jeffers 2005).

First, read to the children, talking about the story and clearly showing the pictures. Your story-telling technique may be to read the story straight through and to show the pictures, or to stop and discuss what is happening and continually gauge the children's level of understanding.

.*Lost and Found* is an effective story to use because the penguin's sadness is misunderstood and then understood by the child and resolved, so that everyone is happy by the end. The child and the penguin embark upon a journey together to find what will make the penguin happy. The child realises that it is his friendship that makes the penguin happy and that being alone makes the penguin sad. You will have a great deal of emotional experience to look at here which the children should be able to understand and empathise with:

- Feeling alone (At one point in the story the penguin and the boy are alone and sad)
- Trying to find the place where you belong
- How friends make you feel safe and happy
- You belong where you are cared for and happy
- You can misunderstand what someone needs (the boy misunderstands what will make the penguin happy and tries to take him home).

1. What the word means – using a character you have told a story about:
   - Before you begin to look at the *word Sad* reiterate that everything ended happily and say you are going to think about what happened to the boy and the penguin in the story. Show the children the card and read the *word Sad* to them. Point out the face on the card.
   - Ask the children what they think the word means and help as necessary.
   - Talk about the story you have just read and ask them what character/s in the story was/*were sad*. "Was the penguin happy at the beginning of the story?"
   - Ask them why they think the penguin was sad.

2. What the feeling looks like:
   - Ask the children to stand in a circle and to think about the sad character, in this case the penguin. Ask them to pretend to be the sad penguin. You might choose a specific, sad moment in the story. There are some expressive drawings of the penguin that you can use.
   - Get half the children to watch the others being the sad character and ask them to describe how the children showed they were sad with their faces and bodies. You can help if necessary by describing the *children's sad* actions (i.e. he or she looks down with straight arms and a sad expression; they stand still or they walk very slowly, dragging their feet along; their mouths are turned down and they don't look at you, only at the floor).

3. Describing the feeling using other words:
   - You can end the process by thinking of other words that are similar to *Sad*, or how you would describe someone as sad in words.
   - Get all the children to pretend to give each other a present that makes them really sad. They might tell you what the present could be. The children might say, "Here is a lovely present for you!" and the others can reply in a very sad way: "Thank you!"

When we are looking at more challenging words like *sad, angry* or *worried*, work through a story in the same way. It is not always safe to say, "Remember a time when you were sad or angry", as this may be upsetting for some children, and it is not always safe to use emotional memory directly. The children will engage with their own experience in a safer way through a character in another medium.

Feelings cards in teaching

> The logic of the emotional mind is associative, it takes elements that symbolise a reality, or trigger a memory of it, to be the same as that reality.
>
> That is why similes, metaphors, and images speak directly to the emotional mind, as do the arts – novels, film, poetry, song, theatre, opera.
>
> (Golman 1996)

You can use the cards very effectively after story-telling to help the children understand the emotional journeys of the character.[1]

The Ugly Duckling, a classic tale of resilience regarding separation, loss and overcoming rejection and fear, is very strong for use with the feelings cards.[2] The "duckling" is, in turn, sad, worried, scared, excited and happy. The children will be totally engaged in the metaphor and you will be using another creature's experience that the children can understand and apply to their own experiences of life. Most children want to be accepted by their peer group, and in the story of the Ugly Duckling he is shunned by everyone but he is resilient and keeps moving and growing, emotionally and physically, until he fulfils himself and becomes a beautiful swan who finds his true place in life. There is a great deal of pain, as well as hope and happiness in this story. If you have looked-after, bereaved or recently adopted children in your class you will need to be careful in your choice of story and work positively towards the success of the character in achieving happiness and their goals. You need to create safety in the work

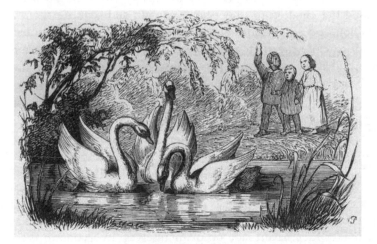

FIGURE 7.1 Feelings cards in teaching: *Ugly Duckling* engraving

and, if you are going to take the journey of a character, be clear that they win out in the end and reach their place of safety. We are giving the children examples and role models in fiction. The child will live imaginatively in the story; you should never underestimate the power of stories and the seeds they plant in the imagination.

Fairy-tales, Greek myths and tales from the Arabian Nights are very strong regarding the characters facing issues that are meaningful to children: *Cinderella* with the loss of her family and the bullying of her sisters, *Jack and the Beanstalk* with a stressed mum and outwitting a giant, *Aladdin* being duped by a family member but winning through and making good choices with his wishes. Many fairy-tales and myths feature characters that experience challenging emotions as they journey through their stories that will have an impact upon children who work through the metaphor.

When you integrate the cards into your teaching you will find other ways to use them. You may put the ones you feel everyone understands on the wall and use them throughout the teaching day. Then feelings become part of how the children understand what they learn. You may use them as you read a story and ask the children to choose a feeling for a character at a particular point: "How do you think Jack is feeling as he climbs the Beanstalk? Excited/worried/scared/eager/thrilled?"; "How do you think Cinderella is feeling after the sisters tear up her invitation? Upset/sad/angry/gloomy?"

If new words are offered you can put them up on your wall. You are creating a living vocabulary of emotions. The wall should be alive for you and in constant use. After a lesson you can point to the feelings cards to indicate how you and the children are feeling.

If an emotion takes place in the classroom you can refer to the wall. Sometimes this may be useful if a child is upset: "I can see you are upset. Let's go to the feelings wall and see if we can find some words to explain how you are feeling."

You can also write down new words, place the "upset feeling/s" on the wall and ask the child to leave it there and take a sad feelings card instead. You are helping the children to understand, contain and regulate their feelings.

When discussing characters and emotions you can talk about feeling different emotions close together, so Jack, in climbing the beanstalk, might feel excited and afraid at the same time. This allows you to open up to the fact that emotions can be complicated and change.

Integrating the cards into activities

If you are using a play activity in an environment you have made such as a shop, hospital, garage or a cafe you can use the cards to say how someone is feeling when they enter your created environment. You have made a cafe and someone comes in to buy a cup of tea. You give this child a feelings card and they must bring this particular feeling into the cafe – they can be a character from a book, a character they have made up or themselves. Everyone in the cafe then has to guess what card you chose by recognising how the person looks and speaks. Let us say the feelings card you gave the child was for *"Sad"*. When they recognise the emotion you could ask everyone in the cafe to be sad. They have "caught" the emotion like catching a cold. When they have done this congratulate them and ask them what they felt about being in *the Sad* cafe. Then let the person come in again and ask the other children to find ways to make them sad. You are now using the cards to investigate how we recognise how someone is feeling and how we can help them. This helps children to develop their empathy and realise that actions can affect and change how someone feels. These little play scenes can be quite short. Go into situations and play with the children – you can be the adult with the poorly pet and get the children to cheer you up. Work with the level of the group: you are playing at situations that might be met in life. Work on scenarios that allow the children to be adults. Do not put them into the position of acting out home-based scenarios, since this might be too exposing for some of them. You will, as we know, get a great deal of information about the children's home life whenever they play freely in the home corner. These exercises are to help them experience life in a safe way as "characters" or "adults". Try some of the following:

- In the vet's waiting room someone has a poorly pet and is *worried*.

- Someone is taking an item back to a shop (ask the children to choose it) because it doesn't work and they are *angry*. The shopkeeper is *scared*.

- Someone *is frightened* about crossing a busy street because they cannot see very well. Help them to calm down and feel confident to cross. (When you are working with the emotion of *fear* it is a good idea to make that person your TA or lead it yourself and empower the children to be able to make you or your TA feel better. They will enjoy being powerful and looking after you for a change.)

Feelings cards (Years 2 to 6)

Split the class into groups of five or six and give each group a piece of paper with an emotion written on it. The complexity of language is in relation to the level of the class you are working with (i.e. *Furious, Bored, Tired, Envious, Worried, Frustrated*, etc.).

Ask the children to discuss the word and for each one to manoeuvre themselves into a position that illustrates the word. Then say "Move" so that they are allowed to move if they want, keeping that feeling. The positions of each child in the group can be different.

- The children have to express that word as a mimed action to the other groups.

- Each group shows their mime to the other groups who try to guess the feeling word that was on the card.

- When guesses have been made the children are allowed to express their feeling in the manner of the feeling word.

■ The children discuss why they guessed the correct word or why they didn't.

When you have completed the exercise ask some of the children to repeat their mime actions and discuss why we understand how someone is feeling from the way they look and stand.

Describing emotions

When you are satisfied that the children understand how a feeling or emotion is shown by the way a person looks, you can then connect the physical attitude with writing. For example, if a child expresses the word "sad" by holding their face in their hands, you could say, "I knew Max was sad because he closed his eyes, hunched up his shoulders and held his face in his hands." Or, "I knew Jessica was excited because she was smiling as she jumped up and down and clapped her hands." You are now moving the children's experience of the feeling word into a description of how that word is expressed by the face and the body. You can now move into vocalising the feeling by giving the children a sentence to say, such as "close the window, it's getting cold". This could be voiced by each group in the emotion of the feelings card and you can begin to discuss how our voices change depending on how we are feeling. Remember: we are always feeling something.

Building vocabulary

You can use the mimed feelings cards exercise to develop vocabulary by giving groups similar words to express and then discuss how the words describe different degrees of emotion. For example:

■ *Furious, Angry, Incensed*
■ *Sad, Ecstatic, Delighted*
■ *Devastated, Overwhelmed, Distressed*
■ *Bored, Remote, Indifferent*
■ *Triumphant, Delighted, Victorious.*

These words become more difficult to mime because they describe the subtlety of feelings. You will discover a great deal about vocabulary and analysing language as you discuss the words' specific meanings and how to express them physically and through vocal tones. Take a sentence such as "I had a test in maths today" and express it in the feeling of the word. Your students may feel that some are similar, such as triumphant and victorious or bored and indifferent, but when you analyse their meaning they are not. This exercise is fun to do and can be a strong starting point for written work.

Applying feelings cards to stories

These exercises work by using the emotional understanding of the child to excite imaginative thinking about the characters. When a child is facilitated to understand and empathise with a character and to interpret the character's actions from the page and into its own experience it will become easier for children to write creatively, as they have become engaged and enter into the story in an experiential way.

The technique with positional drama and the feelings cards is similar. They both help the child to understand and safely experience the life and motivations of the character they have created or are studying. The following model may be used for any story you are studying. You may want to use single elements of the techniques. You can pick-and-mix the ideas to suit your needs. The model is appropriate for all year groups as the teacher uses the same framework and extends it as appropriate to the level of the class.

For Reception, the feelings cards could contain words and drawings/faces. The children might draw these themselves as you retell a story and take them gently through the emotions of the characters.

Model for understanding and writing about a character's emotions/feelings

Jack and the Beanstalk is a very strong fairy-tale because, although an imaginative fantasy, the issues in it relate to many children's experience of life. The story features a boy with a single parent who has to take on responsibilities he doesn't want. He and his mother are poor and she is worried about money, as their farm is not doing well and they do not have enough to eat. Jack has to sell an animal he loves.

Jack makes a bad bargain, in his mother's eyes, when he sells their beloved cow for a handful of beans. He has the courage to climb the beanstalk and meets the frightening figure of the giant, and, with the help of the giant's wife, outwits him. Through defeating the giant and bringing home the bag of gold, then the hen that lays the golden eggs, and finally the singing harp, he rescues his mother and himself from poverty. Jack is a very strong role model for children; they are small in a big world and many have their "giants" to defeat. The giant becomes a metaphor for facing up to things that are frightening or seemingly insurmountable. The metaphor is strong regarding the empowerment of children, as they are able to reflect on what gives them courage, helps them to overcome their fears and face problems.

Investigating emotions in a story (the "Feelings" Detectives!)

When reading the story you can use the ideas we have discussed with regard to the cards to investigate Jack's feelings. Write a list of the feelings cards on the whiteboard and with the children, if appropriate; circle the emotions you think Jack is feeling at different points of the story; for example:

- When his mother tells him to sell their cow at the market
- When he meets the traveller and swaps the cow for beans
- When he is climbing the beanstalk and doesn't know what will be at the top
- When he first sees the giant's castle
- When he first sees the giant
- When he is climbing down the beanstalk and the giant is chasing him
- When he is successful and cuts down the beanstalk after winning his treasure.

You can read the story and stop at any point to ask the children what a certain character is feeling.

You can also suggest that the children raise their hands when they think a character is experiencing a strong emotion and they can circle the feeling word, or write a new one on the board which expresses that emotion. Think about how you engage the children in this process and frame the work as an exciting investigation: what will you find out? You are detectives investigating the emotional profiles of the characters. You are on the trail of the emotional lives of the characters, what they are feeling and why they take certain actions or paths through the story.

Frozen episodes

Set up the above scenes from the story with the children working in groups to discuss how the character or characters will show their feelings. You can look at the feelings of different characters as they interact with each other; for example:

- Jack's mother telling him to sell the cow (the cow can be listening)
- Jack taking the cow to the market
- Jack selling the cow and receiving the bag of beans
- Jack giving the beans to his mother as she realises he has not made any money
- Jack seeing the giant and the bag of gold (the giant's wife helping him to stay hidden or watching out for him)
- Jack giving his mother the bag of gold.

Each of these moments can be a frozen picture from the story. Discuss how the characters are feeling and how they are showing their feelings in their faces and in their bodies. Ask the children to examine closely how the characters look or don't look at each other, if they are smiling, worried or scared, and how they exhibit open or closed body language and how they are sitting or standing in relation to each other. You are working on the children's understanding and analysing of affect (facial expressions) and body language (physical signals of feelings) at the same time as you are exploring the story. This is emotionally intelligent learning; the study of feelings enables the children to empathise with the characters they are reading about and heightens the experience of the learning and excitement of the story. The children begin to understand what it is like to *be* Jack being pressurised by his mother or climbing the beanstalk. They can then write through the emotion of the experience rather than simply reporting the story.

Episodes in action

You can then set up the scene in action and let the children show their feelings in their own words as they portray the situation. Use the same template for the story (this applies to any story you are working on; just break the story down into its framework of episodes).

The children must decide what the characters say to each other during the episode. You can limit it to one sentence each or five or ten sentences, depending upon the ability of the group. The conversation must be clear and tell the story of the episode.

The children work on the episode and you then run them (in sequence) and discuss what you feel about the work with the class. Analyse and build the work as appropriate. The children should begin to learn how to constructively analyse and build on each other's work. When you have worked through the scenes you can run them as a living story board.

The living story board

In both versions you can use the constructed scenes with your class watching and analysing the work and discussing the emotions and feelings enacted in the scene. You can, in a short space of time, create a living story board by giving small groups a sequential episode from the story. You can do this with all the children watching you work with pairs of characters or you can give each group or couple an episode to portray. Use as appropriate for the year group you are working with. The story breakdown can be as follows:

1. Jack's mother tells him to sell the cow.
2. Jack says goodbye to Daisy the cow.
3. On the way to market a man offers to buy Daisy for some beans.
4. Jack goes home and shows his mother the beans. She throws the beans away, but some take root.
5. Jack wakes up and sees a huge beanstalk growing outside his window.
6. Jack climbs the beanstalk.
7. At the top Jack sees the giant with the gold.
8. Jack steals the bag of gold.

9. Jack gives the gold to his mother.

10. Jack steals the hen which lays the golden eggs.

11. Jack's mother doesn't want him to climb the beanstalk again.

12. Jack is chased down the beanstalk.

13. Jack has killed the giant and is back with his mother.

Freeze frame the feelings and write them up on the wall so that the children may experience what it feels like to be Jack – climbing the beanstalk is a good exercise where all the children can mime the action. You can talk them through the experience and go around the class, asking the children to tell you what their Jack character is feeling when you tap their shoulder. You are exploring character, story and emotions in an engaging learning experience. You are investigating character motivation, facing fears, empowerment and dis-empowerment while looking at the structure of the story and building tension and excitement; all of which the children will relate to their own experiences and possibilities.

Teaching emotional and reasoned responses

You can look at feelings (emotion response) and thinking (reasoned response) to Jack's situation. First, look at the emotional response of the character, analysing his feelings when responding to the particular action of the story. Ask the question: "What would you be feeling if you were Jack having to sell his beloved cow at the market?" The emotional feeling response might be: "I really love this cow. I feel so upset and sad about selling her to a stranger."

Once you are sure that the children understand Jack's emotions/feelings you can move into the reasons why he thinks he needs to sell the cow:

■ "We need money for food."

■ "We have no choice."

■ "I have to do what my mother wants."

Other pairings of emotion and reason might be: "What would you be feeling hiding in the castle and seeing the giant holding the chicken that was laying the golden eggs?"– "Frightened at the size of the giant but excited at seeing the golden eggs."

"What are the reasons for you to be feeling like this?" "That giant could kill me with a flick of his finger, but I must get that hen and her golden eggs to buy food when I get home."

You are teaching the children the difference between an emotional response and a reasoned thinking response to situations. To separate these responses is to begin to understand how a character (and ourselves) can react emotionally to situations but also understand how we need to think our way through an emotion to know how to act.

The story of *Jack and the Beanstalk* may be taught for character and story structure but also, at the same time, for emotional learning.

Sound-scapes (across year groups)

Sound-scapes help to build a sense of place by focusing the children's attention in an auditory way on the nature of places and how they sound. The technique may be used in many different ways:

- To help create a living "sound-track" for story-telling
- As a strong preliminary to building vocabulary about place
- To support body mime work when you are using experiential story-telling
- For use with the positional drama models when you are creating place
- When talking about places and how they change (from day to night)
- To help awareness of the use of sound in writing.

Sound-scaping takes children time to enter as a class exercise because it involves confidence and skill. Talk together about the place you are going to create; if it is woodland, talk about the animals and birds, or, if it is a windy or still day; whether trees are being felled or dogs walked. As you work more in this area the children will begin to listen to what sound offers are being made to the "picture" you are creating. You may find it helpful to ask the children to close their eyes so that they can visualise the place you are creating and not be made to feel self-conscious by watching each other as they make the sounds. Encourage them to be sensitive to each other and to listen. Begin with some easy experiments:

- A wood in the daytime and then at night
- The sea
- A storm in a rain forest
- A street in the daytime and then at night.

When you have created your sound-scape ask the children to assess how they could improve it. Play with the sound levels to create mood. You can then lead this aural feeling of place into creating vocabulary with word-scapes.

Word-scapes (across year groups)

Word-scapes are about creating a place using language. When the children offer you language, encourage them to invest the word with a feeling of what it means. They should use their voices in an onomatopoeic way with all the words they make. Go around the class more than once to push the thinking further.

Sit in a circle and give the children the place; for example:

- A Victorian mill
- A desert
- A fridge
- A garden
- A football match.

Extension

Animate the word-scape by getting the children to work in groups to create the object with body mime (see below) and say the words; for example:

- Ask them to make a necklace
- They can all join together and suggest word: gleam, sparkle, shine, shimmer, bling, glisten, flicker, twinkle
- They are allowed to move around
- They must use the language to create the feeling of the necklace.

This exercise is great fun. I have seen remarkable lawn-mowers, aeroplanes and washing machines made by children using this technique.

Body mime

Body mime is a great devise for getting children to enter into working together in a safe way to create something big. It is an adaptable technique that you can develop as you see fit. The children become their own resource to create anything they like with themselves. It may also be used to bring stories to life in an experiential way.

It may be used for:

- Creating places
- Creating objects
- Creating "human sets" for story-telling
- Creating places that can talk.

The premise of body mime is that the children make whatever you need with their bodies: seats, tables, cars or planes and environments.

Body mime exercise 1

- Divide the children into groups of six
- Each group makes something you would find in a house: washing machine, toaster, food mixer, vacuum cleaner

FIGURE 7.2 Teachers experimenting with body mime

- The groups go off to make the object; it must work and have sound
- After five minutes they all come back and show their team the object. The other groups must guess what the objects are.

Analyse

- How did we know what the objects were?
- What improvements could we make? (Add them and watch the work improve.)

Body mime exercise 2

This exercise encourages cooperation and an understanding of physical offers. Stand in a large circle and ask all the children to make you:

- An aeroplane
- A boat
- A fire engine.

The children must go into the middle of the circle one at a time and make a physical offer. The next child then goes in and they build the object child by child. They may talk among themselves if they wish.

Extension

■ Carry out the above exercise in silence.

Body mime exercise 3

Tell a story with the children. It is best to start with a story they all know, such as *Hansel and Gretel* or *Snow White*. You can read them the story beforehand. This exercise works well because you are using the framework of a well-known story.

■ Seat the children in a half circle so that they can become both audience and participants.

■ Tell the story and, as you need things – a door, a chair, a book — the children come up and mime them with their bodies for you.

■ The children can also become characters or animals as necessary and you can either talk for them or ask them to improvise what happens, depending on ability.

Extension

■ You can stop the action in the story and talk about how the characters are feeling.

■ Objects can talk about how they think the characters are feeling.

Experiential writing

Helping the children write through the senses

There is a famous (or infamous) acting exercise where a person becomes a tree. It is often cited as being the silly or daft side of acting, but it is actually used on a deeper level as a metaphor exercise to facilitate the actor's imagination to enter into another experience (Stanislavski 1936). The children must become a tree of their choice and experience what it would be like to be a tree through all their senses:

1. See
2. Hear
3. Feel
4. Smell.

They are talked through a visualisation and take themselves into the other experience.

This working through the senses is a tremendous aid to writing. If we can take children through a visualisation they will imaginatively experience the place they are writing about. You may want to do this to music or in silence. When you talk them through an experience (e.g. Orpheus journeying through the Underworld and crossing over the River Styx), add in, "You are on a black lake in a dark cave. What can you see around you? Reach out your hand. You can touch the wall. What do you feel? As the boat glides along, the oars dip into the water. Does the cave have an echo? Is it deathly quiet? What can you hear? You step out of the boat on to land. What is under your feet? There is a sudden sound. What is it? You begin to walk and the smell of the Underworld hits your nostrils. You can see a dim light – what is waiting for you?" If you lead the children through a visualisation like this they will have a stronger sensual imaginative experience to put down on paper.

8

Strategies for Behaviour

Behaviour is a mirror in which everyone displays his own image.

J.W. Goethe (1749–1832)

There are many reasons why a child behaves in a negative way. A child may have had a bad morning at home or a bad time in the playground. They may be confused, anxious or angry and building towards a level of anxiety that they may not be able to control. For some children their anxiety may come from trauma or a triggered response.[1] In this section we discuss and present strategies and approaches for changing a negative or anxious state of mind or a pattern of behaviour in which the child has become fixed. These interventions will not work in all cases but may prove useful in some.

When a child becomes locked into a pattern of behaviour it is difficult to escape it.

In some cases we should think of a child being trapped into the behaviour by our and their expectations. They carry their last transgression with them; they may feel it gives them a status or an identity. They may want to create chaos around themselves to feel safe. They may want you to react towards them in a negative way, since this confirms their opinion of themselves as "worthless". We know that looked-after and vulnerable children can have "learnt helplessness". This is when a child has gained help because they are unable to do certain things for themselves, namely self-care, socialising or aspects of learning. In time the child learns how to do some of these things for themselves but keeps up the appearance of not being able to do them because they don't want to lose the attention or the support that being "helpless" gives them. They become trapped in a pattern of behaviour which stops them developing and moving forward to greater independence. We need to recognise when children are getting stuck with their behaviours. When we are forewarned by the nursery or the Year 3 teacher that we have a difficult or unmanageable child coming into our class we prepare ourselves for problems. Before we meet the child the die is cast; we are on the defensive and prepared. We might take on an attitude towards the child that will affect our relationship before it has even begun.

Changing states

When a child is locked into patterns of behaviour you will begin to recognise when "trouble is brewing". There may be key factors involved: agitation, rocking in a chair, one-off comments that you cannot quite catch, drumming fingers, humming; in fact a myriad number of attention-seeking activities. Disruptive children are usually attention-seeking children. If you disrupt a class you *will* gain the attention of your teacher. The Changing States Strategy is best described by an incident I observed with my mother and her toddler granddaughter. She had just found her feet and was running too fast and fell over. My mother instantly said as she went to her, "Oh! Did you find a penny?" and my niece, who was about to burst into tears, instantly looked around the floor to find the coin. She had been switched from one state to another by a cleverly placed sentence. She forgot the "state" she was in and didn't enter the emotion of crying but became curious about her environment. This is the Changing States Strategy. You say or do something that breaks the brewing anxious or angry state of mind and tie it into another action or emotion.

Here are a few examples of things to say to a child who you recognise as starting a pattern of negative behaviour. You want to switch their thinking into something else that engages them. They get the attention but you have given it to them for something positive rather than negative. You may decide to have things prepared for this switching: little jobs or messages to be taken somewhere that are important. You could forewarn the office that occasionally a child may come in with a message for a fictitious person and that you are doing this to help control his or her behaviour.

■ "Colin, could you help me to [. . .]?" (Think of a something you need doing.)

■ "Colin, could you take a message to the office for me? It's important." (The message could be: Mrs X will call me at lunchtime. Say I'll call her back.)

■ "Colin, you're good at remembering things — can you remember what we were reading last week?"

■ "The class is getting tired. Let's do a brain gym exercise and wake ourselves up! Colin, what's your favourite one? Let's try it."

■ "Everyone's done really well this morning. Let's have three jokes from the joke book. Colin, pick a number." (The joke book is a good intervention for changing states and energy in the classroom. It is difficult to be anxious when we are all laughing.)

If the class is in the middle of an activity and the child is beginning to exhibit a negative pattern engage them in conversation:

■ "I'm feeling hungry; are you? What's your favourite food? I bet I can guess."

■ "Can you guess what my favourite lunch would be?"

Some of these strategies may need to be prepared in advance, but they will be part of your behaviour strategy and, in time, you will think of ways to involve the child in another activity or engage them with another thought on the hoof.

Always thank the the child for helping you. Raise their status for you and for them.

The technique is not to engage with the behaviour, because the moment you do, the behaviour has become the issue and you are reinforcing the pattern for the child and yourself. You are feeding conflict. What you need to work for is feeding contact and connectedness. Your actions are making an offer to the child not to their behaviour. Imagine the behaviour as a door that shuts the child away from you. The minute you deal with the behaviour the door closes. Deal with the child and the door remains open.

Holding the child's emotional anxiety

This is a use of words and actions to help a child "image" or "picture" their emotion so that you are able to take it and hold it for them. It is an aid to helping the child contain and regulate their emotions. This technique may be used when you recognise that the child is exhibiting attention-seeking behaviour. You may have already noted how the anxiety or anger is building in a child during the lesson; there will often be a pattern of behaviour that you will recognise. You need to acknowledge the behaviour because it is unlikely that the child will stop of his or her own accord. These children may not be able to stop the behaviour because they believe it is out of their control. A child's anxiety will often be invested in an object; for example, they may tap a pencil or bang a book on a desk. If they are investing their anxiety in an object the scenario shown in Table 8.1 may help.

The technique is to identify the behaviour early, and if it is being invested in an object, to take away the object with language that gives a clear indication that you are taking away the feeling that is being placed into the object and placing that object somewhere safe. You are the adult and you can hold the negative emotion or anxiety for the child. If the child relaxes and responds you must recognise and approbate the change in behaviour.

There will not always be an object to use in this way, or the object may be something you cannot take away. In these cases language and demeanour are very important. You must not match the child's anxiety or tone. If a child is trying to goad you into a confrontation the child is powerless if you do not "take the bait" and become louder or sharper in your tone. The child may want to create a confrontation and chaos in the classroom because this is what the child knows and wants to re-create to feel "safe" (see Chapter 3). It is very unusual for a child to want to be singled out and not be part of their peer group functioning happily in the classroom. If you look at challenging behaviour as a "child in trouble" who needs your help you are empowering yourself. You may face these challenges when you are under pressure for time, when you are tired, when you are stressed. Some children, who spend their lives with parents who

TABLE 8.1 Teacher's action table

Teacher's action	What it says to a child	Child's response
1. Calm and smiling: "Colin, you seem to be feeling worried about something. I can see you can't seem to concentrate on the work we are doing. Let me help you out."	The teacher has seen me. I exist, I am important. The teacher wants to help you. No confrontation.	I've got what I want. I'm still angry/agitated/anxious.
2. "I'll hold that book for you. It seems to be holding a lot of anger doesn't it? It must be very tiring for you, give it to me for a while."	I can see you are angry. I am not angry. I am the adult. I can hold the anger for you.	I'm not on my own. The teacher can understand what I am feeling. It does tire me out.
3. Takes book. "Now just give yourself a chance to enjoy the lesson, I know you can have a nice time and can have some talking time later."	I am not alone. She/he isn't angry. I haven't got anyone to fight. She/he will help me.	She/he has taken the book. I can calm down. She/he will help me.
4. Teacher takes book and holds it for a while, then places it on on her desk. Continues to reassure Colin with smiles and nods.	I have absorbed your anxiety. I am taking it away from you.	The teacher can handle my anger. I can have a rest.

suffer from stress and who behave negatively towards them, may well recognise these "symptoms" in you and behave badly when they sense you are edgy and tired. Give yourself this mantra when the behaviour begins to deteriorate: *This is a troubled child, this is a damaged child, I need to help this child.*

You must help yourself to see the behaviour as a symptom of the child's expectations and issues; the behaviour is not the child, it is how the child presents him- or herself to the world for a number of reasons, many of which are not in the child's control.

Rewind

This is a technique used to stop the onset of an escalating behavioural problem. It needs to be used fairly early on when you recognise that a child is having difficulty controlling their behaviour. It literally gives the child an opportunity to start afresh and cancel out the pattern or downward spiral.

Example

Polly comes to class in a temper. She drags her chair across the floor and bangs it down, wanting to attract your attention and disrupt the class. You acknowledge her difficulty and say, "Polly, you seem to be a little angry at the moment. Let's just rewind that behaviour and start the lesson again. Come on everyone, let's help Polly have a positive start to our lesson and walk in with a smile – rewind!" The children all line up again and come into the class as does Polly, who you approbate for sitting down quietly.

All the other children are helping Polly achieve positive behaviour and you end with a "Well done!" to everybody. When you can all rewind together you are working as a team to combat the negative behaviour. It allows you and the child to acknowledge the problem and creates a framework to change the behaviour and make a fresh start. There is also the fun element in "turning time back" which everyone can enjoy. Humour is a great tool for changing states of behaviour. When you are laughing or being made to smile, you change your inner state. It is difficult to laugh when you are anxious or angry.

You can use this technique with one child's action and help them rewind to before they exhibited the negative behaviour. When you have a chance to talk with the children who have the issue with behaviour you may be able to use the rewind as a key to change. When the children are used to it as one of your teaching tools they may even ask you if they can rewind their own or each other's behaviour.

The "yellow card"

This is a way to help children let you know when they are feeling anxious or getting angry. A child's negative behaviour can often seem to come "out of the blue" or change very quickly when it may have been simmering for a while. What we can hope to do is help the child self-regulate (we looked at the way some children have not learned to self-regulate through their parenting in Chapter 1). It is difficult for a child to learn regulation but there may be techniques we can use to help them. If the child can find a word to describe their feeling prior to a "tantrum" this can be very useful. You might help them with this by asking, "Do you feel angry or wobbly or shaky?" The child may identify one of these words with their feelings or be able to give you their word. It is important that the word you find *means something* to the child or the technique will not work. For younger children it is helpful to use a metaphor for the feeling, so you may ask, "Do you see an angry colour?" Or "Do you feel as if you have a lion or a tiger in your tummy/stomach?" When the child can identify the word, object, colour or animal that identifies their feelings of anxiety or anger, ask the child to make it for you. This may be a drawing of a tiger, a yellow or red card or the word "wobbly", or a child with "Worry Pox" as suggested by one nine-year-old girl. It needs to be tangible and lasting, so laminate a picture or a card (you will be using it more than once).

You then negotiate with the child so that when they feel the anxiety creeping up on them they have permission to come up to you, at any time, and whisper the word or pass you the object. When you accept the object you say "I've got it", which will imply that you are now holding his or her anxiety and you can either sit the child with you or your TA can take them out of the class situation. The child must be approbated for coming to you and helped to understand that they are controlling the tiger or the red feeling (i.e. they are regulating their behaviour). "Well done, I'm proud of you, you are the boss of the tiger in your tummy." Anxiety may often come from a child's lack of empowerment in life and their consequent fear of being out of control. You can empower the child through this technique. It needs to be constant and you, the TA or any other teacher who works with the child should be brought into the frame regarding the use of this technique.

The feelings square

Acknowledge the behaviour in an understanding way. You do not challenge it. *You do not give the behaviour the power.* Try to give the behaviour a reason for the child and use the word "feeling" – you are acknowledging the child is in trouble:

- "I can see you are feeling worried about something, Colin."
- "I can see you are feeling sad about something, Colin."
- "I can see you are feeling anxious about something, Colin."

Then approach the child quietly so that you are not giving them the audience of the class, which may accelerate their negative behaviour. It is important that the child gets a moment with you, since their reason for behaving negatively may be to get the focus of the person they perceive as the main "parent" in the classroom. Use the following technique that you can set up with your TA so that you are not drawn away from the class for too long.

- "Let's give you a chance to have a nice time with everyone this morning and put your unsaid feelings somewhere where they can't upset you any more. I want you to go outside with the TA and draw me a picture of how you are feeling. Put it in a box in your drawing and when it's in the box come back in and give it to me so we can put it away for the day. You deserve to have a nice day and I can keep your angry/anxious/worried feelings in my desk."

This exercise is about containment. You are getting the child, with the help of the TA, to put their emotions outside of themselves, look at them, or acknowledge that they are there, and then give them to the adult (teacher) to hold. The TA must be calm and, like the teacher, non-confrontational in tone. You are giving an importance to feelings and to the child's needs but you are always the strong,

147

calm adult. You are modelling an adult behaviour that the child will, in time, find comforting and safe.

The TA draws a thick feeling square so the child is placing their emotions in a contained space. The TA should encourage the child to draw whatever they like. It may be a colour or a scrawl or an animal or words of how they understand their feelings. If the child doesn't want to talk about why he or she feels angry or anxious that is fine. Some children don't understand what makes them angry, and your aim is to calm them down and change their state to one where they are able to engage with the learning and function in the classroom. Obviously if the child wants to talk about something that has happened to them then this becomes a safe opportunity for them to do so with an appropriate adult.

With this technique you are:

- Acknowledging that the child is in trouble
- Giving a powerful metaphorical way to access or get the emotion "out" of the child
- Containing the child's emotional anxieties/fears
- Holding or taking the emotion away from them for a while.

You cannot extinguish it but you can offer them a respite from it.

Once the child has completed the drawing the TA will ask them to fold it up or put it into an envelope (the more you can represent the emotion being contained or closed up, the better). This is the "feelings square". The TA will then ask the child if they would like the TA to give the feelings square to the teacher or if they would like to give it to the teacher themselves. If the intervention is working the child may not want to be focused on by the class when they join it again. If the child wishes to hand it over he or she goes back into the class and hands the envelope to the teacher, who says, "Thank you. I can take that from you now, well done." If the TA returns it the teacher should signal acknowledgement of the achievement to the child and be seen to hold the drawing for a while before putting it away.

After the lesson or during break time the teacher can look at the drawing with the child and talk about the feeling. The teacher should approbate the child for doing the exercise and containing his or her behaviour. You can put the feelings square into place as something the child can do to contain their behaviour and identify when they are working themselves into a state of anxiety, so that they can ask the TA to give them a feelings square to place their emotion in it. If you can work with the child to label the boxes with their emotions they can use them to begin to understand how they are feeling.

It is always important to acknowledge the following when talking to the child:

- "I like you but I don't like this behaviour."
- "I believe you can put this behaviour away in a box and stop it getting you into trouble in class."
- "I will help you be the boss of your behaviour – we can do it together."

FIGURE 8.1 The Angry Lion and the Happy Rabbit: a feelings square

Children with behavioural problems are often isolated by the rest of the class because of their negative influence. You must not isolate them further, even if they are working to make you do this. You must set up a situation where you are working as a team. If the child has a friend who "supports" the negative behaviour then you can try to illicit their help and be a team of three. Interventions with star and behaviour charts are very exposing when a child has trouble regulating their behaviour. An achievement target or a star chart is a passport to failure for children who do not know how to regulate their behaviour. You need to give them techniques and strategies to help them achieve a target.

Traffic lights

This is an intervention that is used in many different forms. The traffic light, an everyday object that many children are taught to trust and obey, is a strong metaphor for safety and controlling impulsive behaviour. It may be used in one-to-one situations but it is also an effective intervention for classroom and playground issues where problems arise between children. Some schools have a traffic light area near the playground where children who have had an argument or a fight can work out their problems with an appropriate adult who is trained in the technique. This is based on a cognitive behavioural model. You recognise the behaviour, swiftly give reasons for that behaviour, look at positive alternatives to the behaviour and what their positive consequences may be, and all agree to put them into operation. The technique will not work as effectively with children who have difficulty in recognising their negative behaviours because they are likely to deny their part in the incident. You need to help them overcome this denial or they will not be able to move their behaviour forward. In some situations when you are working with children who have a traumatic background, it is best to work with them in a one-to-one situation and not as a group exercise, as this can be too exposing for them. The child needs to be able to recognise that their behaviour is negative and needs to change.

When there is a conflict situation you may be posing these sets of questions to the antagonist and protagonist in the situation and, hopefully, when you get to the consequences section the children should be working together.

The progression would be as follows.

Red light – stop the behaviour

- The adult helps the child/children to calm down ("I can see you are angry/upset. You need to calm down so we can talk.")
- The adult asks the child/children to tell them what has happened ("Tell me what happened as clearly as you can.")

Amber light – get ready to change the behaviour

- The adult helps the child or children to recognise the negative behaviour (e.g. "We shouldn't take possessions away, steal, fight, push, call people names.")
- The teacher and the children/child think of other ways to respond or behave in the situation ("How could we behave if someone does that? How can you stop yourself doing those things?")
- The teacher helps the children to think of the positive consequences of new actions ("If we performed those actions what would happen then? Why would that be good for everybody?")

Green light – go ahead and try the new behaviour

- Go ahead and try the best plan ("Do we think this new plan/behaviour is a good idea? Shall we put it into action right now and you can let me know if your new plan works? Well done.")

Ways to talk about controlling behaviour

One-to-one session

When you are talking about negative behaviour don't use language that traps the child in the downward spiral of their negative action. The child may be feeling overwhelmed by negative feelings about their parents, their safety level, the level of their work and lack of ability compared to other children, their feelings of being unwanted, unloved, or just overall "rubbish" (a term used by many vulnerable children when I have worked with them in relation to their view of themselves and their capacities).

When you talk together sit at the same level as them. Smile and adopt an open body position; don't fold your arms or sit back in your chair. Don't write down what they say. If you want to illustrate something use drawings and have a piece of paper between you with pencils on both sides so that they can draw or write down something if they want to. *Empower* them in the conversation with you as much as possible. Use positive language and talk about the behaviour as something that is separate from them that can be contained and controlled. Say that you can and will help them find ways to do this. You are on their side because you think they are worth fighting for.

Questions to ask:

- "How can we help you be the boss of your behaviour?"
- "Can you *feel* when you are beginning to wind up inside?" (Use the metaphor of a spring tightening and then letting go.)

If they can identify when they are getting anxious you can use this to suggest interventions – the yellow card may be useful here.

- "What ways can we catch your bad behaviour before it gets too big?"

Take offers from the child for this and use any that you think might work. If they do not have ideas you can offer your own techniques to try (one at a time – talk them through the following techniques and then agree to use one next time their behaviour turns negative).

1. Rewind technique
2. Yellow card technique
3. Feelings square technique

Drawing is a good idea – because children talk better when something else is happening between you that takes the pressure off a face-to-face conversation.
Ask the child to draw an outline of themselves on a piece of paper.

1. Ask them to draw things they like to do around themselves. This can be hobbies initially, so that it is relaxed and not connected to school.
2. Then ask them to draw what they like to do in school – don't lead or make suggestions unless they offer nothing. They may draw a football, being in the playground, PE, etc. Talk about what they offer, and show you are interested in them.

3. Ask them to look at the drawing of themselves and picture where they feel their negative energy is building up – it might be their stomach, chest, head or hands.

4. Ask them to draw something in the place where the negative energy builds up – offer the coiled spring or draw an animal. If they give you a word you can write that down in the relevant position.

5. Ask the child to draw what happens when the wound-up feeling gets out of control.

6. Draw a box on the paper (if there is room) or on another piece of paper. Ask the child to draw or write in the box something that represents their feeling. This could be a colour, animal, word or object. Let the child lead. Talk about the metaphor or word they choose. Help the child understand the emotion through what gets put into the paper square.

7. Take the square and cut it out. Say this will become the object the child can give you or the TA when they are feeling a negative emotion. It will be a code that will let you know what is going on for the child; the minute he gives it to you he is no longer alone in fighting the negative feeling.

8. Agree that you will use this card as a way to be boss of the behaviour. Say what will happen when the child gives you the card (you may let him or her go out with the TA, sit near to you, or just acknowledge that you will hold the behaviour and be watching to help the child control it).

9. Laminate the card and put the plan into action.

This method enables you to build an intervention together; it is a private code. This is powerful for the child and helps build a positive relationship between you. When the child uses the intervention, approbate and congratulate them. Do not allow it to become ordinary or take it for granted. Revisit the word and the feeling. See if you can help the child contain the emotion and make it smaller. You are working to contain the emotion and regulate the child's reaction to it. When he or she gives you the card they are making enormous strides forward in their emotional lives; it is a crucial part of their learning life skills.

Notes

Introduction

1 Latin: in place of the parent.

1 The Secure Base – Attachment to Learning

1 Social and emotional aspects of learning.
2 Boys Town continues to flourish in the USA, giving care to 400,000 children (boys and girls). It was founded as an orphanage for boys in 1917 by Edward J. Flanagan, a Roman Catholic priest working in Omaha. The "City of Little Men" pioneered and developed new juvenile care methods in twentieth-century America, emphasising social preparation as a model for public boys' homes worldwide.
3 Children Act 1989: S31(9).
4 See the following section on Bowlby's Theory of Attachment.
5 See Chapter 3.
6 See Chapter 3.
7 We look in greater depth at the behaviour of children who have suffered trauma in Chapter 3, and at behavioural strategies in Chapter 8.

2 Emotional Intelligence

1 Bertrand Arthur William Russell (1872–1970), British philosopher, logician, mathematician, historian.
2 "Satisfactory is not good enough" (Ofsted framework, April 2009).
3 It appears that emotional arousal following a learning event influences the strength of the subsequent memory for that event (Silva *et al.*, 2007).
4 The ability of leaders to understand that, in order to ensure that others will follow their lead, they must gain their respect and support.
5 Irish poet and dramatist (1865–1939).
6 Marcus Tullius Cicero (106–43 BC), statesman and lawyer. One of Rome's greatest orators and prose stylists.

3 Teaching Vulnerable Children

1 Carl Gustav Jung (1875–1961), Swiss psychiatrist – the father of analytical psychology.
2 The Explanatory Memorandum notes:

> Vulnerable children are defined within the Order [. . .] to relate to the needs of a diverse range of children: any child in need (including disabled or very sick children), children on the periphery

of care, in care, or who have left care. It is drafted so as to include support to parents who may need help for their mental health, substance misuse, learning disability, poverty or other problems that may affect a child's opportunities and wellbeing.

3 "Acute stress response" was first described by Walter Cannon (1915).
4 Thalamus: Greek θάλαμος = *room, chamber*, function includes relaying sensation, special sense and motor senses to the cerebral cortex.
5 Amygdala: Greek *amygdalē*, meaning "almond". An almond-shaped group of nuclei in the forbrain. It performs a primary role in emotional responses, response to threat and emotional memory.
6 Pre-verbal abuse: when a child suffers trauma before they master language.
7 Delay in all areas of learning.

4 Experiential Drama

1 Project for Adopted Children with Gloucester Social Services Adoption Service Team (2004).

5 Positional Drama

1 The Ripples Project (1996). Tetr Wybrzeze Gdansk Poland Education Project in partnership with University of Northern Iowa, USA.
2 Leonid Leonjon.
3 Charles Dickens, *Oliver Twist*, Chapter 46, "The Appointment Kept" (The Spy Under the Wall).
4 London's first police force.

7 Emotional Learning in Class Delivery

1 Vihelm Pederson, *The Ugly Duckling*. Andersen's first illustrator.
2 Hans Christian Andersen, 1843 (Andersen said the story "was a reflection of my own life").

8 Strategies for Behaviour

1 As discussed in Chapter 3.

Bibliography

Ainscow, M. (1995) "Education for all: making it happen". *Support for Learning*, 10(4): 147–154.

Alban-Metcalfe (2001) *Managing Attention Deficit/Hyperactivity Disorder in the Inclusive Classroom: Practical Strategies for Teachers*. London: Fulton Publishers.

Balbernie, R. (2010) *An Infant Mental Health Service*. The Child Psychotherapy Trust.

Beatty, B. (2000) Keynote paper, "The paradox of emotion and educational leadership", given at BELMAS Conference, Bristol.

Bodine, R.J. and Crawford, D.K. (1999 [1969]) *Developing Emotional Intelligence: A Guide to Behavior and Conflict Resolution in Schools*. Champaign, IL: Research Press.

Bowlby, J. (1969) *Attachment and Loss*. London: Pimlico.

—— (1989) *The Making and Breaking of Affectional Bonds*. London and New York: Routledge, ch. 6.

Braithwaite, J. (1989) *Crime, Shame and Reintegration*. Cambridge: Cambridge University Press.

Brandon, M., Thorburn, J. and Rose, S. (2005) *Living with Significant Harm: A Follow Up Study*. London: NSPCC.

Brighouse, T. (2006) *Essential Pieces: The Jigsaw of a Successful School*. London: Sage.

Cairns, C. and Stanway, C. (2004) *Learn The Child. Helping Looked After Children to Learn*. London: British Association for Adoption and Fostering.

Cairns, K. (2002) *Attachment, Trauma and Resilience. Therapeutic Caring for Children*. London: BAAF.

Cannon, W.B. (1915) *Bodily Changes in Pain, Hunger, Fear and Rage: An Account of Recent Researches into the Function of Emotional Excitement*. New York: Appleton.

Carter, R. (1999) *Mapping the Mind*. New York: Phoenix.

Cawson, P. (2002) *Child Maltreatment in the Family*. London: NSPCC.

Cooper, P. (2004) "Is 'inclusion' just a buzz word?" *Journal of EBD*, 9(4): 219–222.

DCSF (2009) *Delivering the Behaviour Challenge: Our Commitment to Good Behaviour*. London: DCSF. Available online at http://publications.education.gov.uk/eOrderingDownload/DCSF-00961-2009.pdf.

DfE (1994) *The Education of Children with Emotional and Behavioural Difficulties*. Circular 9/94. London: DfES.

DfES (1998) *Social Inclusion 10/98–11/98*. London: DfES Publications.

Elton Report (1989) *Discipline in Schools*. Report of the Committee of Enquiry. London: HMSO.

Frederickson, N. and Cline, T. (2002) *Special Educational Needs: Inclusion and Diversity*. Buckingham: Open University Press.

Fullan, M. (1993) *Change Forces: Probing the Depths of Educational Reform*. London: Falmer Press.

Fullan, M. and Hargreaves, A. (1991) *What's Worth Fighting For? Working Together for your School*. Toronto: Ontario Public School Teachers Association.

Gardner, H. (1983) *Frames of Mind: The Theory of Multiple Intelligence*. New York: Basic Books.

—— (1993) *Multiple Intelligences: The Theory in Practice*. New York: BasicBooks.

—— (1999) *Intelligence Reframed*. New York: Basic Books.

Gardner, H., Kornhaber, M. and Wake, W. (1996) *Intelligence: Multiple Perspectives*. Ft. Worth, TX: Harcourt Brace College Publishers.

Gerhardt, S. (2004) *Why Love Matters — How Affection Shapes a Baby's Brain*. London and New York: Brunner-Routledge.

Ginott, H. (1971) *Teacher and Child: A Book for Parents and Teachers*. New York: Macmillan.

Golman, D. (1996) *Emotional Intelligence*. New York: Bantam Books.

Hawkins, K. (2010) "Emotional intelligence in the primary school". Interview, 8 and 12 February.

Hernstein, R. and Murray, C. (1994) *The Bell Curve*. New York: The Free Press.

HM Government (2008) *National Domestic Violence Delivery Plan: Annual Progress Report*. London: HMSO.

Hughes, H.M., Graham-Bermann, S.A. and Gruber, G. (2001) *Resilience in Children Exposed to Domestic Violence*. Washington: American Psychology Association.

Jeffers, O. (2005) *Lost and Found*. London: HarperCollins Children's Books.

Killick, S. (2006) "SI32 Management of anaemia in MDS". *Transfusion Medicine*, 16: 20.

Kounin, J.S. (1970) *Discipline and Group Management in Classrooms*. New York: Holt, Rinehart & Winston.

Kyriacou, C. (1991) *Essential Teaching Skills*. London: Blackwell.

MacBeath, J. and Mortimore, P. (2001) *Improving School Effectiveness*. Buckingham: Open University Press.

Maslow A.H. (1956) *Towards a Psychology of Being*. Vol. 1, edn 3. New York: John Wiley and Sons.

—— (1968) *Towards a Psychology of Being* Volume 1. New York: John Wiley & Sons.

—— (1970) *Motivation and Personality*, edn 2. New York: Harper.

Mason, M. (1996) "Alliance for inclusive education". *Guardian*, 18 June.

Miles, L.K. (2009) "Too late to coordinate: Contextual influences on behavioral synchrony". *European Journal of Social Psychology*. First published online.

Myers J.E.B. (2002) *The APSAC Handbook on Child Maltreatment*, edn 2. London: Sage.

O'Hanlon, C. and Thomas, G. (2004) "Editor's preface", in Skidmore, D. (ed.) *Inclusion*. Buckingham: Open University Press.

Provence, S. and Lipton, R. (1976) *Infants in Institutions Revisited*. New York: International University Press.

Robertson, J. (1998) *Effective Classroom Control: Understanding Teacher–Pupil Relationships*, edn 3. London: Hodder & Stoughton.

Rogers, B. (1994) *Behaviour Recovery: A Whole School Program for Mainstream Schools*. Harlow: Longman.

—— (1997) *Cracking the Hard Class*. London: Paul Chapman.

—— (2002a) *Teacher Leadership and Behaviour Management*. London: Paul Chapman.

—— (2002b) *Classroom Behaviour: A Practical Guide to Effective Teaching, Behaviour Management and Colleague Support*. London: Sage.

—— (2004) *How to Manage Children's Challenging Behaviour*. London: Paul Chapman.

Rogers, W. (1991) *You Know the Fair Rule*, edn 2. London: Pitman Publishing.

Save The Children (2010) *Measuring Severe Child Poverty in the U.K.* London: Save The Children.

Scott-Baumann, A. *et al.* (2002) *Becoming a Secondary School Teacher*. London: Hodder & Stoughton.

Sharma, N. (2007) *"It Doesn't Happen Here" – The Reality of Child Poverty in the UK*. Ilford: Barnado Press.

Silva, A., Kirshner, S., Brown, R., Josselyn, S., Han, J-H., Cole, C., Neue, R. and Guzowiski, J. (2007) Researchers Unlock Key to Memory Storage in Brain. *Science Daily*. University of California: Los Angeles. Available online at http://www.sciencedaily.com/releases/2007/04/070419140914.htm.

Skinner, B.F. (2002) *Beyond Freedom and Dignity*. London: Hackett Publishing.

Sroufe, A., DeHart, G.B. and Cooper, R.G. (1998) *Child Development, its Nature and its Course*. New York: McGraw-Hill.

Stanislavski, C. (1936) *An Actor Prepares*. Translated by E.R Hapgood. London: Methuen.

Stansfield, V. (2003) "Bill Rogers: a practical guide to effective teaching". Review. *Journal of EBD*, 7(4): 241–249.

Steer, A. (2009) *Learning Behaviour: Lessons Learned – A Review of Behaviour Standards and Practices in our Schools*. London: Department for Education. Available online at http://publications.education.gov.uk/eOrderingDownload/DCSF-Learning-Behaviour.pdf.

Steer Committee (2006) *Practitioner Report on Learning Behaviour*. London: DfES Publishing.

Teacher Development Agency (2002) *Qualifying to Teach Standards*. London: TDA Publications.

Sternberg, R. J. (1985) *Beyond IQ: A Triarchic Theory of Human Intelligence*. New York: Cambridge University Press.

Turner, C. and Scott, S. (2004) *Community-based Crisis Services for Young People: An Evaluation of the Mental Health Foundation Programme, 2002–4*. Report.

UK Action For Children (1994) *A Survey of Women*. London: UK Action For Children.

Walker, A., Flatley, J. and Kershaw, C. (eds) (2009) *Crime in England and Wales 2008/09. Vol. 1, Findings from the British Crime Survey and Police Recorded Crime*. London: HMSO.

Winfield, L.F. (1994) *NCREL's Urban Education Programme*. Urban Education Monograph Series.

Index